RAISING ALL BOATS

VICTOR EDOZIEN

RAISING
ALL BOATS

MY JOURNEY OF
AMERICAN ENTREPRENEURSHIP

Published by Advantage, Charleston, South Carolina.
Member of Advantage Media Group.

ADVANTAGE is a registered trademark, and the Advantage colophon is a trademark of Advantage Media Group, Inc.

Printed in the United States of America.

10 9 8 7 6 5 4 3 2 1

ISBN: 978-1-59932-739-6
LCCN: 2018948094

Cover design by George Stevens.
Layout design by Melanie Cloth.

This publication is designed to provide accurate and authoritative information in regard to the subject matter covered. It is sold with the understanding that the publisher is not engaged in rendering legal, accounting, or other professional services. If legal advice or other expert assistance is required, the services of a competent professional person should be sought.

Advantage Media Group is proud to be a part of the Tree Neutral® program. Tree Neutral offsets the number of trees consumed in the production and printing of this book by taking proactive steps such as planting trees in direct proportion to the number of trees used to print books. To learn more about Tree Neutral, please visit **www.treeneutral.com**.

Advantage Media Group is a publisher of business, self-improvement, and professional development books and online learning. We help entrepreneurs, business leaders, and professionals share their Stories, Passion, and Knowledge to help others Learn & Grow. Do you have a manuscript or book idea that you would like us to consider for publishing? Please visit **advantagefamily.com** or call **1.866.775.1696**.

To my mother, Mary Ego Edozien

TABLE OF CONTENTS

INTRODUCTION

My story is the chronicle of an American student of Nigerian descent with an accent, a stutter, and one hundred dollars to his name who managed to get a great education, to save and borrow enough capital to buy a business, and to start and run an investment group that turns over hundreds of millions of dollars in revenue each year. It is a story that could only happen in America, where the sum of a man's efforts, ingenuity, and even good fortune count for more than who he knows, the color of his skin, or what he was born with. I have driven my own success, but I've also been blessed by the kindness of strangers. Each time I reached a dead end and thought I might have come as far as I would be allowed, someone—a teacher, a priest, a banker, a mentor, or someone inspired by the will or hand of God—gave me another chance. I know it was God's will for me to proceed and carry on with my goal.

I believe I've made the most of every opportunity. I also believe that as the recipient of kindness and second chances, I have an obligation—a calling—to offer those things to others. In a world where being an entrepreneur can mean anything from incubating a brilliant tech innovation while still in your Harvard dorm and launching it as a $100 billion IPO to buying a food truck with your last dollars and toiling day and night to turn your investment into a means of feeding a family, I've had to define entrepreneurship for myself. My concept of entrepreneurship isn't focused primarily on maximizing personal wealth. It's focused on creating value—for me, for my customers, for my employees, and for our communities. It is an interpretation of entrepreneurship that is inseparable from a commitment to the greater good.

I often encounter a difference, which seems to be rooted in race, in how entrepreneurship is perceived. In many minority and some immigrant families, and especially in families of African descent, not a lot of credit is given to individuals who choose the risky path of entrepreneurship. Our parents want us to go to college, get good grades, find respectable jobs, start 401(k) accounts, buy houses, and live comfortably until we retire. It's a path of security above all else, and there is a notion in much of the African American community that it is the individual in the corporate world, rising through the ranks, who is the most valuable, positive reflection on his or her community.

I believe there is a higher calling than even the honorable path of corporate success, and that calling is to innovate, to create value, to solve problems, and to engineer opportunities for the people and communities who need them most. It is a calling to raise all boats by enabling entrepreneurship to benefit a workforce and a community.

In my experience, when you do all those things and deliver economic value to communities, personal success follows.

This is the story of my uniquely American journey of entrepreneurship and the lessons I've learned along the way.

PROLOGUE

In December 2004, I bought my first factory, a dying electrical parts manufacturer in Harbor Beach, Michigan. The business had been one of more than a dozen plants owned and operated by an auto industry supply conglomerate. One by one, the factories had been shuttered, the jobs shipped off to Mexico, Honduras, and China. Harbor Beach was the last factory standing. Its employees had endured round after round of layoffs, and by the time I became involved, only a skeleton crew remained. Those men and women knew the doors of their plant could close forever on any given day, and that seemingly inevitable end would likely mean long-term unemployment. There were no other jobs in their small industrial city.

After closing the deal, I went to the factory to speak with the workers alongside my CPA, Mike Onianwah, who was also a childhood friend.

When we arrived and walked onto the plant floor—two black men with Nigerian accents in a town with a 98 percent white population that had long been preparing for more bad news—the facility went silent. All eyes were on us. I'm sure the employees thought the end had finally come for their factory and their jobs.

I took a deep breath, mindful of the transaction I'd just completed, in which I traded my life's savings for the chance to turn this business around. Then I introduced myself to the group and delivered the news that might have been the very last thing they were expecting to hear: "I've never run a manufacturing plant before, but I believe I have a way to turn this place around if you are willing to work with me."

Chapter 1

BORN IN THE USA

The world belongs to optimists; pessimists are only spectators.

—Francois Guizot

No matter how I tell my story, one of the most important facts of my life is that I was born in America. My parents, both Nigerian, were students—my father studying electrical engineering at Cornell, and my mother earning her master's degree in zoology at Rutgers. We lived in New Jersey for the first few years of my life, though I have very few memories of it. I was just a kindergartner when we moved to the suburbs of Lagos, Nigeria, but my US citizenship would one day be my passport to a new life.

In America, my parents were just two foreign grad students, but in Nigeria they were Edoziens—and my father's family name implied both influence and affluence. Lagos is a huge metropolis of more than 20 million people—more than some entire African countries. On its outskirts, there are a handful of suburbs that are as vibrant, eclectic, and prosperous as the suburbs of any major city in the world. We lived in one of these—Ikoyi. My siblings and I grew up in its bubble of highly educated, wealthy, well-traveled, and well-heeled residents. It was a place where most of the homes had servants, where families belonged to country clubs, and where kids attended private schools. Houses like ours were surrounded by high walls topped with razor wire, and we had a manned gate and a night watchman. Where I grew up, children were either born rich or born poor, and most lived their entire lives in the same social condition in which they were born. Later, when I moved to the United States and started a new life, a life without the wealth or privilege I'd known in Nigeria, I would learn firsthand how different things can be in America—what life can be like when you aren't defined almost exclusively by where you come from or your father's name.

Because we lived in Ikoyi's unique enclave of educated people, where the neighbors included expats and members of the diplomatic corps from all over the world, we were constantly exposed to Western culture. English was my first language. I read the same comics and watched the same movies as kids in every Western city in the world. (When I was little, my favorite was *Casper the Friendly Ghost*, but as I got older, I became a big *Spiderman* guy.) Most summers, we traveled to London to visit my mother's sister, and while we were there we hung out with other expat kids, seeing the same friends and cousins every year. My father rarely accompanied us on these trips, and they were happy, relaxed times.

I had a few friends at my private school and a few others in the neighborhood, including Deji Kehinde, who had an American mother and a Nigerian father. We played soccer and tennis together and swam in the country club pool on hot afternoons. Aside from a few occasions with my neighborhood friends, my happiest childhood memories are of my time in the Boy Scouts. I did as much as I could with my troop, attending meetings, learning knots, working on survival skills, and camping when it was offered.

My father had a good government job, and my mom was a virologist in a lab that designed and manufactured vaccines. As a boy, I knew there was more to Africa than our little cosmopolitan corner of Lagos, but it wasn't something I thought about much.

My childhood may sound idyllic, but it was not as peaceful or appealing as its setting. Every child struggles with something, and I was no exception. At home, my parents provided two very different kinds of influence. My mother was patient and thoughtful, and she was devout in her Catholic faith. Every Saturday, she took us kids to confession to reflect on and repent for our sins, and every Sunday—without exception—she took us to Mass. Even as a small boy, I could see how those services calmed my mom. She found her peace in the church, even though her marriage was at odds with the most basic of Catholic tenets. She had married a man who had two other wives and children from many different women.

My father was unlike my mother in almost every way. He was impatient, imperious, and a strict disciplinarian. My memories of my childhood with him are of being fearful and wary. When I was young I thought that this, like his polygamy, was just the way things were. But as I got older, I saw that many of my friends' and cousins' fathers were gentler and would never lay a hand on their children.

Sometimes I wondered if the fact that he had so many children was the reason my father didn't seem to have enough time or affection for any of us. We lived on a compound with a main house and smaller houses on the grounds. At any given time, there was only one woman living in the main house with my father. Siblings came and went. I was close to many of them, but others I didn't know as well. Most of my friends were from families comprised of one husband, one wife, and their children. It didn't make sense to me that my father, a man who had gone to Cornell, lived this life with many children from different wives.

As a boy, I was awkward and introspective, nearsighted, asthmatic, prone to nosebleeds, and afflicted with a speech impediment. Kids would tease me about my glasses, about the shape of my head (though my mother assured me it was fine), and most of all about my stutter. There were times when I couldn't get the words I wanted to say out, and if I got upset, it got harder. I'd take deep breaths, trying to force the words through, but it was a constant, frustrating struggle. I'd listen to other kids at school, kids who seemed to be born with the gift of being able to just start speaking and have their words flow. I could never do that. I always had to think ahead and choose my words carefully, avoiding ones that gave me trouble.

It didn't take long for me to realize that it was more difficult for me to start speaking with some words than with others. Some got stuck in my throat and wouldn't come out. Unfortunately, my name—Victor—was one of these. At school, when a teacher would ask the students to introduce themselves, I'd panic. The last thing I needed was for the other kids to be looking at me, waiting, and thinking, "He doesn't even know his own name." I had to learn to keep calm as my turn neared and remember to start with an easier word. If I led with, "My name is ..." then I could introduce myself without looking foolish.

Despite my struggles with speech, I was an excellent student. When I was ten, my father decided to send me to boarding school, as was the tradition in our family. Two of my brothers were already attending a school near Lagos, so I thought I'd be sent to the same place, but instead I was enrolled in a new government-run secondary school in Idoani, a rural area six hours from home.

My mother helped me pack and drove me to the middle school in Idoani run by the federal government. The roads narrowed and the scenery became sparser as we approached. There was only one road through the town, with cassava and vegetable farms spreading out for miles around it and a small town center with tin-roofed houses set close to the road. We saw fewer cars and more bicycles as we neared. The air was dusty. The school was only in its second year and didn't have a lot of infrastructure yet—just a small collection of low, colorful buildings that served as classrooms, boys' dormitories, and girls' dormitories. A hard lump grew in my throat as I surveyed the grounds and looked at the rudimentary campus and back at my mother. In my family, no one defied my father, but I couldn't understand why I'd been singled out to be left in this place.

I trudged through the arrival process, accepting my green and white uniforms and then taking my things to the dorm I'd been assigned. I'd share with three other boys, each of us in a bunk with a small locker at the bottom for our belongings. I met the young house captain who would chaperone us from place to place. I stayed composed as I said goodbye to my mother, but for days after, when it came time for lights out in our dorm, I pulled the sheet over my head and cried. Up until then, I'd never spent a night away from my family, and suddenly I was completely alone. I had no phone access, so I wrote letters to my mom. She tried to visit once each term on visitors' day, but it was a long time between those visits. When she couldn't come, one of my aunts who lived a little closer came to see me.

My father never visited in the five years I was at the remote school he'd chosen for me. It was a difficult time, but looking back, I believe it was also the beginning of my emotional self-reliance. With so much distance between my father and me, I began to feel I didn't need his validation for my choices.

When the rainy season gave way to the dry season, my asthma worsened. In Lagos, the damp ocean breeze keeps irritants down throughout the year, but in Idoani the wind blows in from the desert, and my throat constricted when I breathed in the dust. I had an inhaler, but as the weather became more arid, I had a severe asthma attack and had to be taken to the school's clinic. It kept getting worse, and the inhaler wasn't helping. As I sat in the clinic office, wheezing and coughing, an administrator decided my condition was too severe for the school to handle. A school employee loaded me into a hired car, and I spent the next six hours with my inhaler in hand, struggling to breathe. When we arrived in Lagos, the driver turned me over to my mother, who took me straight to the hospital. I was hospitalized for three days.

When I recovered, I was sent back to school. From then on, I'd only see my family during summers and holidays.

Despite the remote setting, my classmates came from all over the country, representing a cross section of ethnicities and religions. There were other boys like me at school, kids who'd never been on their own before, and so we learned to survive together. I started out sitting in the back of every classroom, praying I would not be called on—and that if I did get chosen, I would not stutter—but a math teacher who was kind to me and put me at ease made it easier for me to move up and participate. I couldn't play soccer because my distance vision wasn't good enough, so I joined the basketball team and was soon the sixth man. The school had a newly founded scout troop, so I became one of its first members. On Sundays, the Catholics went to Mass together, and I found comfort in the service that was the same in Idoani as it had been in Lagos, in London—everywhere I'd ever been. I made friends, and some of those guys are still my friends today. We were only ten years old, and we only had each other. The first two years were lonely and difficult, but after that it got better. I became a good student and leader. By the fifth year, I was chosen to be a prefect—a student appointed into a leadership position with discipline authority and extra responsibilities over other students.

When I was fifteen, I took a college placement exam and received a high enough score that I was eligible to enroll in college early. I wanted to study electrical engineering like my father had, but in Nigeria, each program of study has a quota of students who are allowed from each region and ethnic group. My region already had enough electrical engineering students. I was informed that if I wanted to, I could begin my university studies immediately in geology instead.

I had mixed feelings about going. The university was on the other side of the country, in Port Harcourt, hours from home. I had no interest in becoming a geologist. And even though I wasn't especially self-aware, I knew that at fifteen, I was young. The idea of being so far away from home again—this time among boys who would all be older and more experienced than me—was intimidating. But my dad wanted me to go. He placed great importance on education, and he saw an opportunity both for me to get ahead in my studies and for my academic skills to reflect well on him and the family. My mother was hesitant, but she had little say. I had to obey my father.

Academically, I was ready for the university. Socially, I was not. I was in a dorm with boys who were two and three years older than I was—most of them were already eighteen. There were so many things they knew and had already experienced that I hadn't encountered yet. I was just a kid—a Boy Scout—and I was out of my depth.

One of the things that helped me acclimate to life on campus was finding a positive outlet for my energy. I may not have known what an entrepreneur was back then, but I already had a desire to create something original and profitable. A few boys and I formed a club called the GEM organization. Our goal was to bring emerging and established recording artists to campus. We'd charge students a small fee and book acts we'd all like to see. My role was to liaise with road managers and make sure the technical side of each show—things like power, lighting, and sound—ran smoothly. Over the two years I was at the college, we managed to host four concerts, including one by Mandy Brown Ojugbana, who had a hit record in Nigeria. We made a little money, and I got my first taste of entrepreneurial success.

Unfortunately, even though I'd found one activity that kept me engaged at school, it wasn't enough. In every other area, I was struggling. My grades weren't as good as they should have been. My friendships were tenuous. I started hanging out with a group of students who were more into recreational drugs and parties than classes. I was in over my head, and eventually I started to feel like if I didn't make a change, I would lose what little control I had over where I was headed. Two years into my university studies, instead of registering for classes, I moved back home not sure what I would do next—return to school, transfer to another school, or get a job after spending time at home.

Back in Lagos, though, things were no better than at school. In the time I'd been gone, my parents' marriage had become strained, and the tension between them was thick and toxic. My mother tried to hold her own, but my father pushed and bullied and threatened to get the obedience he wanted from her and from us. I could feel the pressure building in our household and within me.

I was not the only one of my father's children to respond poorly to this development. One of my sisters argued with my father and moved out. She came home one day looking for some of her things and found the storage room locked. When she asked if I knew where the key was, I gave it to her. By the time my father came home, my sister was gone, and he lashed out at me for helping her. He hit me so hard his ring flew off his hand; then he locked me in a bathroom. For two days, I was not allowed to leave, and my father instructed the rest of the family—including my mother and brothers—not to speak to me. A steward who worked for my father brought me one meal, but other than that I had no food and no human contact. Whatever my dad's argument with my sister had been, I took the brunt of his anger. At the end of the second day, the steward unlocked the door and told me I could leave. My father never mentioned the incident again.

I decided I couldn't stay home any longer. I could not openly defy my father in his house, but I could not continue to subject myself to his erratic and sometimes brutal treatment, either. I packed my passport and a small bag with some clothes. I knew I wouldn't be able to get far without money. My father's briefcase often contained cash in different currencies for his business, but I didn't know if I dared to take anything from him. I thought about how he'd tormented me and mistreated my mother and about the dark fate I felt waited for me back at school. I could not see any other options. I was seventeen, and I felt like I was being pulled down a path I did not want to travel, as if I had no control over where my life would go. I didn't want to grow up to be the kind of man my father was, with his many wives and his bullied children and a career that was built on the strength of his name. I wanted to make my own way.

What I did next made it possible for me to wrestle my fate back under my own control. I am not proud of it, and I have often thought about the consequences for me, for my mother, and for my younger brother. While my father was away, I snuck into his office, opened the briefcase, and stole an envelope of money. That night, I slipped out of the house, bought a one-way plane ticket to London, and left Lagos. It would be six years before I would see Nigeria—or my father—again.

———

In London, I went to visit friends from my previous summers in England and was invited to stay with one family and then another. After a few weeks, I went to see my aunt—my mother's sister. I didn't dare call home, but I wanted my mom to know I was okay. My aunt and my cousins told me it was time to go back, but I never considered it. I believed my father would kill me if I returned.

After I let my aunt know I was unharmed, I tried to keep my distance from my relatives in London. I missed the comfort and familiarity of my aunt and her home, but I was afraid that if I kept in touch through her, my father would think my mom had somehow played a role in my running away. He might even think she was helping to support me. Either way, it would make things harder for her; I didn't want to be responsible for any more damage than what I'd already done.

At first, my stay in the United Kingdom was like the summers of my childhood. I had a bunch of friends to hang out with and stay with for short periods of time. I spent my days playing soccer, watching movies, and visiting friends. I looked at a few colleges but quickly realized that as a noncitizen, I would have difficulty enrolling in any UK school—as well as an impossible time qualifying for any financial aid. For the same reason, I couldn't get hired for any job.

Among the people I was hanging out with, there were three distinct groups: those who were living a temporary life of leisure, with their parents footing the bill; kids who were working hard day in and day out to make ends meet; and kids who were somehow on the dole, receiving a small income from the government that kept them in food, clean clothes, and rent-subsidized council flats. I had always been in the first group—the group who was just having fun and didn't have to worry about money—but I was not a part of that life anymore. I didn't fit anywhere.

I needed a plan that would allow me to finish school—that was all I was sure of during the months I was in London.

Even though I was relying on the kindness and hospitality of friends, by late fall I was nearly out of money. I had enough left for a single plane ticket. Maybe I would not have run away if I wasn't afraid of my father, or maybe I would have gone back. But I was terrified. I believe, more with each passing year, that parents should be a point of last refuge, no matter how bad the world gets. But there was no refuge with my father; and I knew my mother—graceful and intelligent and dignified as she was—would not be able to protect me if I went back to Nigeria.

My only other viable option was to go back to the United States. I was a citizen, and if there was any place I could figure out a way to go to school, I would find it there.

With the last of the money I'd taken, I bought a one-way ticket to New York and a connecting flight to Syracuse, where the only person I knew in the United States—my childhood friend Deji Kehinde—lived. After paying for my trip, I had about one hundred dollars left.

I hadn't been to America since I was five years old. I was scared that I wouldn't be able to find a place to sleep, scared that I would run out of money and go hungry, and terrified that no American college would take me, but I had chosen this path, and I was going to see it through. As the plane descended into New York, I bowed my head and prayed. I remember thinking, over and over: *I just have to keep going.*

LESSON I LEARNED
Run Your Own Race

If there's one thing my childhood taught me, it was that relying on validation from others was a losing proposition. Maybe it was because I was a middle child, or because my parents didn't get along, or maybe because I was a unique combination of academically capable and socially challenged. Whatever the reason, I learned that it's okay to feel lonely; that there's nothing inherently wrong with feeling like an outsider; and that if I just focused and stayed determined, I would find a way to get where I wanted to go.

As an entrepreneur, you can't burn all your energy trying to earn acknowledgment from anyone—investors, friends, parents, competitors. So many people feed off of validation and lack any sense of direction without it, but an entrepreneur should look inward, not outward, for approval and learn to value substance over status.

Focus on your goals, strive for the accomplishments you believe matter most, and find your own happiness. None of this means you have to cut yourself off from the world—that's never a good strategy. But it does mean you have to free yourself from everyone else's expectations and standards to figure out what really matters to you. You have to run your own race, and what matters most in that race isn't necessarily being the fastest or the first; what matters is making progress over time, always moving toward your own goals on your own terms. As a boy and as a young man, I was just beginning to learn this lesson, but with every year that passes I am more certain that it is valuable both as an offense and as a defense for any entrepreneur.

Chapter 2

WORKING CLASS

*Pray as if everything depended on God. Work
as if everything depended on you.*

—Saint Augustine

arrived at John F. Kennedy International Airport in February
of 1987 with a vague plan that involved becoming a student at
Syracuse University and studying engineering. The first shock
of New York was the weather. I'd never seen snow like they had in
Syracuse, and I'd never been that cold in my life. There were days
during that first month when the high temperatures were in the
single digits and the wind was so bitter and icy it seemed to suck the
air out of my lungs when I stepped outside. My teeth chattered and

my feet went numb. I wondered if maybe I had chosen the wrong place, but it was too late to turn back.

I had chosen Syracuse because Deji was there. He was living with relatives near the university and working nearby. I took up residence on his sofa, and his family welcomed me. At first, they thought I was on a holiday, but after a few days I told Deji the truth: I was staying. My plan was simple but profoundly lacking in detail: get a job, enroll in the university, and earn my degree without any help from my family.

Deji looked at me like I was crazy, then shook his head. "Well then," he said, "you need to get off my couch and get a job. You can't just stay here and watch TV." He told me I'd need an ID, a Social Security number, references, and experience.

I was willing and ready to work, but I'd never had a job before. In Nigeria, my parents had always emphasized education, not work. My father's house was a rich one, with house help and a cook. The only chore my mother made my brothers and I do was make our beds. When I went away to boarding school, my basic needs were met there, too. At the end of each week, we'd put dirty laundry in bags at the ends our bunks, and three days later the clothes would reappear, clean and folded. I'd never prepared a meal, never washed a dish, never cleaned a bathroom, and never done a load of wash.

But whatever I had been before, I knew that was over. I had come to America as a poor young man—not yet even a student. I was well aware that I was stepping onto the lowest rung of the class system. I just hoped there would be a place for me to stand.

In England, I exchanged letters with my sister Annette, knowing she would have an update for me about my mom and would be able to let her know I was okay. The news from home was devastating. My father had kicked my mother out of his house. She'd spent almost twenty years with him, and he'd sent her away with two suitcases and her last-born son.

I wanted to help them, but I had nothing to offer.

Annette wrote that ever since I'd run away, my father had been telling the rest of the family that my mother and all her children would end up in living on the streets in America, that we would amount to nothing.

Annette encouraged me to focus my anger and frustration and my worry over my mother's situation into making something of myself. She told me to work hard, stay out of trouble, and most of all to go to school. This was a mantra in my family, where having a degree was an integral part of family identity. It was part status and part insurance policy—we all presumed that with an education, we would always have access to good jobs.

My father's spiteful words were enough to push me to succeed, but I had a long way to go. I had my etiquette and my background of privilege, but I had no skills to help me get a job.

As the winter started to give way by small measures, I got hired at a car wash, making two dollars for each vehicle I cleaned. On days when the temperatures got above freezing, I washed cars by hand, keeping track of my day's tally by putting a pebble from the gravel lot in my pocket for each vehicle. One evening, after a couple weeks of hand-scrubbing cars in the cold, I went to the owner for my day's pay. She paid me for nine cars, even though I'd washed ten. I was positive of the count. When she argued, I took the pebbles from my pocket and counted them out on the counter, believing that this was a mathematical error, rather than the swindling of a powerless employee. The boss was not impressed, and she refused to pay for the tenth car. I couldn't believe the injustice of it, so I quit.

When I got back to Deji's house and told him about how unfairly I'd been treated, he was furious—with me. He couldn't believe I'd quit my first paying job. He demanded to know what I was going to do next.

By that time, I had gotten my Social Security number, so I tried job hunting through a temp agency. They sent me out to work as a janitor at a local community center. I didn't tell them I'd never cleaned anything before. I figured I would learn on the job.

On one of my first days, the senior janitor told me to mop the gym floor. I got out my supplies and did as I'd been told. He stood watching me for a few minutes, and then asked me the obvious question.

"Son," he said, "haven't you ever held a mop before?"

I'd been found out. I was not qualified for the job. I looked up at him and shook my head—a barely perceptible acknowledgment— then continued pushing the mop around the floor. I couldn't believe I was about to lose another job. But instead of calling me out—or getting me fired—he said, "It'll take you all day to clean it that way. Let me show you how they taught us to do it in the Navy."

That day he taught me how to mop, and in the days that followed, he taught me all the other cleaning tasks I had to know to keep the job. I paid close attention and worked hard.

At the community center, while I was mopping the floors and washing the windows and water fountains, I looked around me and saw families like mine. I thought about my mother and my brothers and wondered where they were and if they were okay.

At both of those first jobs—and at many of the other part-time positions I held later, as a student—I was acutely aware of the way people saw me. (Or didn't see me, since occasionally people acted as if I wasn't even there.) They saw a foreigner with dark skin, heard my accent, and knew I had no money. Some found it easy to overlook me, as if I was invisible.

But for every person who was dismissive, there was one who was kind. Another of my earliest jobs was at Norstar Bank, where I was hired through a temp agency to file checks. My supervisor complimented me on my work one day and asked about my background. She seemed genuinely interested in my history and in my aspirations to earn a college degree. After that day, she always requested me from the agency and gave me as many hours as I could use on the weekends. The job was perfect, most notably because it was on the main bus line, so I could get there easily.

After a month of graciously hosting me, Deji's family was ready for me to move on. In fact, both of us moved on. Deji took a semester off and got a full-time job and an apartment, and I rented his spare room. I was earning just enough to cover the cost of my bed and the roof over my head.

As soon as I established a work schedule, I walked to the Syracuse campus and found the registrar's office. The school was intimidating, with its huge, hundred-year-old stone buildings and thousands of students. This was a very different type of college from the one I attended in Nigeria, and I was not coming to it as an academic prodigy. I didn't have anything but my determination to recommend me. Still, I reminded myself that my father went to Cornell and my mother to Rutgers, and I asked the admissions counselor what I had to do to enroll.

The counselor politely asked if I had taken the SAT, and I didn't know what that was. She asked if I had any college credits to transfer, and I said I did, but when she requested a transcript, I didn't have that either. I had no record of my two years of university studies in Nigeria. I didn't even have a high school diploma. As we reviewed the list of documents I did not have, I began to realize how unlikely it was that this prestigious university would consider a student like me.

I felt a rising panic. I had run away for this. I had stolen from my father and left my mother and my kid brother behind. My departure had been the catalyst for a lot of hardship for them. I had rebelled, and we had all paid a price. I knew I might never be able to make it up completely, but getting an education—proving myself—was going to be my start. If I could not get past the scrutiny of the admissions office, I didn't know what I could do to make things right for myself or anyone else.

The admissions counselor listened to my story and recounting of the classes I had taken, and instead of turning me away, she said I could enroll in University College. This division of the Syracuse institution was designed to cater to part-time students and members of the community who wish to take courses. The program made a limited number of classes available for non-matriculated students at a lower cost than regular university courses. If I did well, the counselor explained, I could earn my way into a degree program.

Even at the less expensive tuition rate, University College classes cost $300 per credit—so I would have to figure out a way to come up with $900 for each class. Between my jobs at the community center and the bank, I was working forty hours a week at just a little over minimum wage. I could barely cover my meager living expenses. I did the math and realized that I only had enough savings to cover a single credit—one third of one class. I would have to find a way to live on less.

Each weekend, I made my way to the Alibrandi Catholic Center on campus to attend Mass. As a child, I had attended church because my mother told me to, but now that I was alone, I found that the services helped me feel calm and centered. Mass was the same as it had been in Nigeria, and the chapel on campus came to feel like a refuge.

That December, I spent my first Christmas on my own. It was a stark reminder that the path I had chosen was a lonely one. I worked the entire day to earn some extra pay.

The first classes I took came easily to me, as I had already taken equivalent courses during my studies in Nigeria. They were general education subjects: introductory math, English, and writing. By the end of my first year at University College, I had passed enough courses with high marks to earn admittance as a full-time, matriculated student. Now I could qualify for financial aid.

After one more semester with good marks, I was admitted into the electrical engineering program. At my class's orientation into the engineering school, one of the professors announced, "I want you to look at the person to your left and the one to your right. One of the three of you will not be here at graduation." It was a warning about how rigorous the program would be, and I remember doing my best to keep my eyes straight ahead in that moment, because I was sure the students on either side were looking at me.

It was around this time that my transcripts finally arrived from Nigeria, and even though I had never had an interest in geology, I would have hated for the credits I'd earned to go to waste. I met with a counselor to go over my records, and even after she had eliminated all the credits that were ineligible for transfer, I was well on my way to earning a geology degree. With the blessing of my advisor, I began pursuing it as a second major. I had gone from being an outsider on campus to having homes in two departments.

Dr. Peter Plumley, a professor in the geology department, took an interest in me after class one day, asking me about my background and my studies before coming to Syracuse. When I explained about my dual major and my early studies in Nigeria, he invited me to sign on as an assistant in his research in paleontology/geology. Like the bank manager, Dr. Plumley let me work flexible hours, and I was able to add his work-study position to the two jobs I already had.

———

Academically, I did well. I wasn't at the top of my class, but my fears about washing out of the engineering program seemed unfounded. Even though I was working constantly and receiving financial aid, though, it wasn't long before a tuition bill that I couldn't pay came. I made an appointment at the financial aid office to see if there was any more help available to me, but the counselor wasn't sympathetic.

"Everyone wants a Mercedes," she told me as we went over my paperwork, "but not everybody can afford one. Maybe you just don't belong here at Syracuse. Maybe you should try a state school or a community college, instead."

She was probably right. I had no right to an education at this prestigious university, but I was committed. Syracuse had become my home in America. I'd made a few friends. I'd found an ally in Dr. Plumley and work that allowed me to keep up with my classes. The idea of starting over somewhere else felt impossible.

The counselor said there was nothing she could do for me. I left her office and went to the chapel. I knelt in one of the pews and started to pray. For the first time since I'd arrived in Syracuse, I doubted I would be able to get through. I prayed for a way to stay. I couldn't believe it had come to this after I'd finally earned a place at the school.

While I was sitting in the church, Father Borgognoni came and sat beside me. He asked me what was wrong, and I told him how I'd run out of chances at the university. He talked with me a while, and then we knelt side by side and he prayed with me. When I stood up to leave, I thanked him and bowed my head. He put his hand on my shoulder and told me to have faith, that God had a plan for me.

As I left the chapel, he said, "Victor, tomorrow I want you to go to the bursar's office and try one more time to straighten this out."

In the morning, I trudged across campus to the bursar's office, steeling myself for another lecture about how I was just not wealthy enough to be a Syracuse student. Instead, when I asked for help with my account, I was informed that the campus Catholic Charities organization had paid the balance of my tuition for the semester.

LESSON I LEARNED
Have Faith

It was not until I was a student at Syracuse that I truly began to understand the connection my mother felt with the church and its role in her life. All my life, I'd seen her find contentment through prayer. Even when things were terrible between her and my dad, she would go to the church and pray, and she would come home renewed and at peace in a way that came from within—as if the worries of the world couldn't touch her.

As a child, I was drawn to the ritual of religion, but in college, I began to feel what my mother must have felt all along—the tranquility that comes with faith. In the years since, I have come to view my faith not just as part of my deeply felt religious belief, but also as a central tenet in the way I approach everything in my life, including business decisions.

Sometimes situations don't go my way. Sometimes my intuition is bad. But ever since my years as a student at Syracuse, I have absolute faith that things will work out the way God intends them. I have been blessed with skills and opportunities, and I have encountered devastating failures. I look at everything that has happened to me, and I know that it is all larger than one man and his choices.

As an entrepreneur, I make my decisions with careful deliberation and thought. But when I choose a path, I do so with zero doubt. God opens doors for me, and even when it seems there is no way to move forward, he shows me a way.

Chapter 3

FOCUS ON THE MISSION

To succeed in your mission, you must have a
single-minded devotion to your goal.

—Abdul Kalam

After finishing my semester with the help of the Catholic Church, I knew I had to figure out a way not just to graduate but to pay for the rest of my education. One night I heard a TV ad about enlisting in the army. By the time it got to the part about earning money for college and the enlistment bonus, I'd decided I had nothing to lose. I called the recruiter, and when he heard my accent, he asked if I was an American citizen. I told him I was, and he offered to pick me up the next day. At his office, I took the Armed Services Vocational Aptitude Battery test and got a high enough score that the recruiter recommended I also apply for the Reserve Officer Training Corps. I signed up for both programs.

In the summer of 1989, I shipped off to basic training. The group of us leaving from the area showed up at 4:00 a.m. at the massive Federal Building in downtown Syracuse and stood outside as the recruiter passed out plane tickets. After we landed in Atlanta, we caught a bus to Fort Benning, Georgia. The minute the bus arrived, drill sergeants started screaming at us—to get off the bus, to grab our gear, to move faster. They shouted, *"Let's go!"* and *"Move it!"* and, to anyone who hesitated, *"What don't you understand about that?!"* They got too close, standing nose-to-nose with us and screaming in our faces. Sometimes two of them would stand on either side of a recruit, yelling in tandem. They singled out recruits who were slow, chatty, confident, cheerful—and sometimes their choices just seemed random. I guess they wanted to shock us, to let us know that things had changed completely from wherever we came from.

In the processing center, I stood in line to have an initial physical, get my head shaved, receive my gear, and have blood drawn. The next day, as we stood waiting to depart for the training zone, a drill sergeant stood in front of us reading off the names of recruits who needed further blood work. The guys had been talking about this list—the HIV list. I knew very little about HIV, but I'd heard people say it came from Africa, and I came from Africa, too. I was as scared in that moment as I'd ever be while I was in the army. I didn't know if I had the virus in me. My serial number ended with "038," and the drill sergeant read out a number that sounded just like mine. The last digits were 0 … 3 … 9. That guy was called to the medical office and we never saw him again.

I thought I'd learned a lot about hard work since I'd taken my first job washing cars, but I was completely unprepared for the army's version of a long, hard day. On the first morning, we were up at four, with a drill sergeant screaming at us until my newly shaved head was pounding. We ran and did calisthenics every morning before sun-up, and it seemed that we couldn't get anything right. Whether we were getting off a bus or running or gathering our gear, we weren't good enough or fast enough, and the drill sergeants let us know it.

The first time I took the physical fitness test—a timed assessment that included push-ups, sit-ups, and a two-mile run, I failed. That was a first for me—to not make the cut, to not measure up. It forced me to reflect on what I was capable of and on how hard I was willing to work to succeed. I threw myself into my morning workouts. By the end of week three, I was able to pass the test—doing seventy push-ups in two minutes, more than eighty sit-ups, and running two miles in under seventeen minutes. Those numbers were the army's minimum standard, but they were a huge accomplishment for me.

I quickly learned that the only good answer to 99 percent of the comments and questions directed to me was either, "Yes, drill sergeant," or "No, drill sergeant." I also discovered that the color of my skin and my accent meant nothing whatsoever to the army. On the very first day, one of the drill sergeants stood in front of our company and cast an appraising look over the group.

"By the time you leave here, we are going to make *soldiers* out of you," he bellowed. "I don't care where you are from, what color you are, how you speak, or how you look. Every one of you is army green to me—and you *will* all be soldiers."

It didn't take long for the drill sergeants to show they were true to their word. When some of the recruits started separating themselves into groups based on ethnicity, home region, and other shared backgrounds, the drill sergeants stepped in to break them up, shuffling squads to keep us mixed. They wanted us *all* to rely on each other—not just those who had something in common outside of the army.

Under constant direction and frequent aggression, we started to pull together as a unit. During the first weeks, we sweated through our predawn workouts together, marched together, ate together, got punished together, took classes together, and were drilled day in and day out on the army's core values. From there, we moved on to the shooting range, where we learned to assemble, disassemble, clean, and shoot our rifles with deadly efficiency.

One of the most difficult days of my basic training was the day I had to learn how to shoot. I was born with severe nearsightedness in my right eye, but because I am right-handed, I was supposed to look through the scope of my M16 with my right eye. With my vision deficiency, I couldn't see the target. While my peers completed their qualifications one by one around me, I struggled to hit the target at all.

My drill sergeant came up and looked me over. "*You're* right-handed," he shouted. "*You* can see. *Why* aren't you hitting that target?"

I explained about my nearsightedness, and he offered a solution: he would make me a left-handed shooter.

Like most right-handed people, I had never used my left hand as the lead for any activity. I had to outfit my rifle with a deflector to redirect empty rounds from hitting me (or the soldiers beside me on the range) in the face. Needless to say, I had to spend a lot more time on the range to meet my qualifications than almost anyone in my training company. Even after most of the recruits finished their marksmanship requirements, I had to head back out for another day of shooting. It was blisteringly hot and dusty, and everyone in the group that went out with me had also failed the range qualifications.

I was determined to get through it, willing my left hand to be more dexterous and responsive. By the end of that remedial day on the range, I had not only exceeded my minimum qualifications but had also earned the next level of marksman proficiency—a sharpshooter medal.

Once I'd finally learned to handle my rifle, I moved on with my training company to face the one trial nearly every recruit fears most: nuclear, biological, and chemical (NBC) training. The army doesn't just teach recruits about these kinds of weapons by talking about them. It exposes them to CS gas, which is sometimes used for crowd control, so they'll have some idea of what to expect and how to react if they ever encounter toxic gas. As a group, my squad put on our gas masks and learned to operate them. It felt like trying to breathe through a plunger. Then our drill sergeants led us into Fort Benning's gas chamber and lined us up against the wall. They ordered us to take our masks off and put our helmets back on.

The gas in the air burned my throat and skin, and I tried to keep my eyes tightly closed. It felt like I was going to suffocate. All around me recruits were coughing, retching, and gasping. I could feel hot tears on my face as the gas seeped into my tear ducts. The drill sergeants, still wearing their masks, asked some of us questions and even made a couple recruits recite the soldier's creed. Even in agony, we did as we were told. Finally, they told us to face right and for each recruit to reach out with his left hand and put it on the shoulder of the soldier in front of him. Then, blindly hanging on to one another, we stumbled out of the chamber. The exercise was terrible, but it taught us how to make sure our masks were on and sealed properly. It was a skill that could be a lifesaver.

After a short break, we had to go back into the chamber—this time not wearing our masks, so we could practice putting them on under pressure. The goal of gas chamber training, like the rest of basic training, was to teach us to maintain our focus no matter what was going on around us.

Near the end of our training, we experienced one of the other best-known and most-anticipated events of basic training: the night infiltration course. It's an obstacle course recruits have to complete in the dark—while live rounds fly over their heads and controlled explosions happen all around them. I remember crawling on ground and looking up, thinking, *My God, I am a soldier. If I stand up right now, I'll die.* When I made it to the far side of the course, my heart was pounding, and as I looked back across at the tracer rounds streaking over the field, all I could think about was whether any kid ever panicked out there and stood up—and if so, if he had survived.

As hard as basic training was, once we got past the do-or-die days in the beginning, I realized that I was thriving within the structure the army gave me. Every single thing we did in basic training that summer, in the combat training I attended the following year, and in all the drills and workouts and training year-round with ROTC, was mission-oriented. We were never, not for one minute, allowed to forget that we were soldiers, and as soldiers our job was to focus on our mission.

Being indoctrinated into this culture of total focus and singular purpose was a turning point in my growth as a young man. By the time I finished basic training, I felt like a different person. I was disciplined and confident. I was self-aware. And I was strong, down to less than seven percent body fat and able to easily meet the army's demanding physical requirements.

I felt like I could do anything.

LESSON I LEARNED
Approach Goals with Discipline, Focus, and Consistency

Flying home from Fort Benning, I pivoted my focus. With basic training behind me, school was my new mission. I no longer doubted that I would graduate. Everything else was secondary, and I knew beyond question that I was willing to make any necessary sacrifice.

By the time I volunteered for the army, I had made a few friends on campus, and many of those students were working multiple jobs, slogging through their school work, and living the same moment-to-moment kind of life I'd been living before I enlisted. Many of those acquaintances ended up dropping out of school; it was just too difficult to meet all the obligations that were required to finish. If I hadn't joined the military and gone through basic training, I could easily have taken that path. But once I was not just a student but also a soldier, I never considered it.

So many times in our lives, the difference between success and failure is simply a margin of self-discipline. As an entrepreneur, you must recognize that fact and be willing to commit as much of your resources, time, and energy as necessary to get a job done. Your mission may change from year to year and decade to decade, but your commitment to it should never flag.

Chapter 4

GRADUATION

Education is the most powerful weapon which
you can use to change the world.

—Nelson Mandela

One of the basic tenets of most engineering schools is that they are designed to be exclusive. To ensure that reputation, many schools make it ridiculously hard to get through the curriculum. It's almost an educational philosophy, and Syracuse was no exception. They fully expected a third of us to fail.

At first, it seemed I might be among that third. My lower-level engineering courses were far more challenging than I'd anticipated, but I was lucky enough to have a professor early on who pointed out where I was coming up short. After handing back one of our exams, he pulled me aside to tell me he thought I was struggling with the basic calculus theories and applications I needed to understand.

He was right. I was studying, but up until that semester, all the math classes I'd ever taken had emphasized rote memorization over understanding concepts. This was especially true in Nigeria, where memorization is held in the highest regard as a learning tool. I knew the mechanics of the math, but I didn't understand the reasoning behind it.

I took my professor's advice to heart and enrolled in more math courses, starting with Calculus I and II during the next two semesters. Outside of class, I went to the math study tables three times a week to work through the areas where I had knowledge gaps. At the study tables, graduate assistants helped students identify and overcome deficiencies. When I started to truly understand the math—not just how to solve it, but the logic behind the formulas and their implementation—my grades went up. As a bonus, by the time I fully grasped the calculus I needed to do well in the engineering curriculum, I'd accumulated enough courses to earn a minor in mathematics.

Another area that challenged me throughout my college career was writing. As someone who had always struggled to speak fluidly because of my stutter, I had made a tenuous peace with the language that involved speaking briefly and carefully, and I wrote in the same manner. I took a literature course in my second semester and had to write a long paper. Thinking that language is all about vocabulary, I got a thesaurus from the library and sat down for a long evening of finding "better" words than the ones I knew for what I wanted to express. The whole paper felt stunted, as if I had stuttered my words onto the page in terse sentences full of overreaching words. When I got the essay back from my professor, he'd circled most of the words I'd found in the thesaurus and written *"Why?"* beside each of them. I got the point, but I remained uncomfortable with expressing my thoughts on paper—a process that still rattles me today. I've found that PowerPoint presentations are better suited to my strengths—bullet points are the challenged writer's friend.

My biggest trial in the classroom was the one I'd been struggling with my whole life—my speech impediment. I sat in the back and kept my head down, always praying I would not be called to speak in front of the class. When I was chosen, I often froze. One of the things a stutterer learns over time is that a lot of people inappropriately assign meaning to our hesitation. If I couldn't blurt out an answer quickly, the other students—and sometimes the professor—would assume I didn't know it. I often *did* know what I needed to say, but I couldn't express it quickly enough to prove it.

Another thing people commonly associate with stuttering is dishonesty, so if someone asked me a question like, "Did you troubleshoot the electrical system?" my hesitant reply might be taken as a way of getting out of answering the question—rather than the simple but frustrating gap between my thoughts and my ability to express them that it really was.

As a result of my speech challenges, I was one of the quietest students in my classes. I only spoke up when I absolutely had to.

Because of the financial pressure on me and the difficulties my mother was facing, I knew I had to graduate in the shortest amount of time possible. So outside of my eight weeks of basic training and six weeks of advanced infantry training the following summer, I went to school year-round. Some semesters, I took eighteen or even twenty credits, and in the summer, when terms are designed for a student to take one class at a time, I doubled up. Through it all, I worked two and sometimes three jobs. After I'd completed basic training, I got a job as a guard with Burns Security. I could work two twelve-hour shifts on the weekends with them in addition to my other jobs. Because I was a contractor, I got sent to all different kinds of job locations—sometimes for a few weeks and sometimes for a few months or longer.

One of my early assignments was at a food distribution company that had trucks coming in and out all through the night and early morning. That was a tough job, mostly because my station was in an outside guard shack, and I had to walk rounds through all the buildings every hour. Working in a tiny outdoor guard shack during a Syracuse winter was a hardship that paid a little more than some of the easier assignments. Despite the extra money, I preferred indoor jobs, especially since they occasionally allowed me a little time to study between my duties. My supervisor was supportive of my efforts to put myself through school, and when he could, he assigned me jobs where I could bring my books and squeeze in a little study time. Sometimes, when a visitor would check in at my station, he or she would notice my books spread out behind the counter—electrical engineering, advanced math, and geology texts—and look at me with surprise.

"Are *you* an engineering student?" a few asked.

I'd tell them that yes, I was studying for two degrees at Syracuse. After that, many of them would wish me good luck before heading on their way. To this day, I do a lot of my best work late at night, a habit I attribute to my days behind the security desk.

In addition to my security job and my research work-study in the geology department, I got a second work-study job in the university's audiovisual support department. Since I frequently had gaps of an hour or two between classes, I used that time to race across campus to set up projection equipment and AV materials for classes in different academic buildings. It was an ideal opportunity to squeeze in another fifteen hours of work each week.

My work in the AV department offered the added perk of giving me exposure to all kinds of classes I was not taking as a student. If a professor needed someone to stay in the lecture hall to run a presentation, I often volunteered and got to observe whatever art or history or architecture the students were learning that day on top of my own studies.

At Syracuse, my core group of friends was largely composed of international students. Even though I am an American, people didn't really look at me as one because of my accent and foreign upbringing. I had friends from Holland, Egypt, Liberia, England, Afghanistan—all over the world. There was something beautiful about that group and its myriad perspectives, and there were a lot of people who enjoyed hanging out with us because of that diversity. There were some in the group who were elitist, carrying around notions of Americans being ignorant, but the fact that we were all students at a top university on American soil seemed to inherently prove them wrong.

It was true, though, that I was still sometimes misperceived by people who didn't know me. One year, I went with a girlfriend to her family's home in Connecticut for Thanksgiving. We were sitting around their table when her grandmother passed me a platter of meat. I took a portion and turned to the person next to me, but she put her hand on my arm and said, "Oh, no, take more. Where you're from I'm sure you don't eat like this."

I didn't know what to say, but my gut reaction was to take offense. The idea that anyone who looked or sounded like me was starving was insulting. This person somehow thought she knew me based on what she'd seen on TV or read in magazines. But my girlfriend put her hand on my knee and pinched me, hard, under the table, and I stayed quiet.

As that day wore on—and even more as the years passed—I thought a lot about the intentionality of that comment and others like it. The grandmother wasn't being unkind; she wanted to feed me. I had to learn to accept that just because someone was unaware of my background didn't necessarily mean they were mean spirited.

I experience this same kind of unintentional prejudice even today. Every once in a while, when I kneel to pray in church, a woman in front of me glances back and sees her purse beneath me on the pew—and she can't help but grab it and move it away. I have been pulled over for no greater offense than "driving while black" so many times I've lost count. In each case, I have to make a decision, and I usually choose to give the benefit of the doubt and assume the person stopping me is trying to prevent crime, not willfully committing a racist act.

———

In the spring of 1991, I graduated from Syracuse University with a BS in electrical engineering. At the end of the summer term, I completed my BA in geology with a minor in mathematics.

Syracuse holds convocation for each of its schools and then a general graduation. At the engineering school's convocation, the students, our dean, and our professors gathered in an auditorium for the ceremony. Sitting there listening to the dean speak, I was reminded of the first speech I'd heard in the same room, two years earlier—the one where our professor told us to look left and right and to know that one of the three of us would not make it.

When the dean called my name to walk across the stage, I was supposed to shake his hand and pose for a photograph, then move on. I was so elated that when my turn came, I just stood there holding his hand, grinning out into the crowd. That was my moment, and I didn't want it to end.

Ever since I'd finished boot camp, I'd known that I would make it, but countless people I met along the way thought I would fail. I'd been told I couldn't afford it; that I couldn't get through; that I wouldn't be smart enough or sufficiently determined. My own father had told my extended family I'd never accomplish anything in America; that I'd end up living on the streets. But for every person who doubted me, there was someone else who believed in me and built me up, like the bank manager who gave me a flexible schedule and extra hours, the priest who consoled me and miraculously helped me secure a tuition grant, and the professor who took me under his wing and gave me the chance to do paid research. With their encouragement, I had defied the odds and accomplished the first, biggest goal I'd set in coming to America: attaining a university education. I had arrived in Syracuse as an immature, ill-prepared, penniless kid, but I was walking off the convocation stage as a graduate, an engineer, a soldier, and a self-made man.

A day later, my mom and my younger brother Frankie arrived to attend the main graduation ceremony at the Carrier Dome. It was the first time I had seen my mom since I ran away, and I was overwhelmed with emotion. It meant so much to me for them to be there. They had just moved to New York, and after four years of being on my own, I felt like I had a family again.

If I had stayed in Nigeria, I might have finished my education in geology and used my family name to get a government job. If I'd remained in my father's good graces, I might have been granted some measure of financial security and status in his circles. I might have become a man who lives behind a ten-foot wall topped with barbed wire, like he did.

Instead, I ran away to the only place I've ever known where the actions a person takes are more critical to success than his or her birthright. Even though there are pockets of American society where financial security is derived primarily from family, there are many other ways to get from a low point to a high one. The most effective of these is education. Education, combined with hard work, changed my life's trajectory. The education I'd strove and fought and sacrificed for had lifted me from an outsider who was just a hundred dollars away from becoming indigent to a guy with a world of possibilities ahead of him and the beginnings of a lifelong love of learning.

LESSON I LEARNED
Know Your *Why*

My experiences as a student taught me how critical it is to see the big picture in my studies and in my work—to understand the *why* of my problem solving. If I had stayed focused on the minutia of one class at a time, I might never have gotten the math support I needed to become successful in engineering. Over the years, I've come to realize that deliberately choosing to take a broader perspective, looking at the reasoning behind both processes and people, has served me well as both an employee and an entrepreneur. Understanding the reasons behind the decisions that are getting made, behind the way a company does business, behind who gets hired and who does not, and behind who succeeds and who fails makes me a better person, a better businessman, and a better employer.

When you encounter a situation where you don't feel like you have all the information you need to make an informed, thoughtful decision, dig deeper to figure out what you're missing. The search for that absent component, and the understanding that comes with getting at elusive information, is almost always worth your time and effort.

Chapter 5

WORKING WORLD

Someone's opinion of you does not have to become your reality.

—Les Brown

After graduating from Syracuse, I was able, for the first time
in years, to breathe easy. I was no longer juggling multiple
part-time jobs and as many classes as I could handle.
Through the university's placement office, I interviewed with several
companies and received multiple job offers. The trajectory of my
life had completely changed. Instead of being in a position where I
needed to accept any employment I could find (and as much of it as
possible), I was starting to build a career.

There were two things that were important to me in choosing my first engineering job. First, I wanted to have a role in making something. Even though my degree was in electrical engineering and could have led to more theoretical projects, I felt compelled to choose an industry with a tangible end product. Second, I didn't want to be part of anything destructive. Despite my service in the army and my pride in that experience, a job with a defense contractor that recruited on campus didn't appeal to me. I wasn't keen on spending months at sea on an oil rig, either, which ruled out a job with Atlantic Richfield Company. In the end, I gratefully accepted a job with Carrier Corporation. They had an excellent rotational engineering program, they made a useful product (air conditioning systems), and I would be based in Syracuse, which had come to feel like home.

For the first time in my life, I had a job that paid well. The first thing I did was buy a sporty car with headlights that popped up from the hood. I rented a townhouse. I went to the mall and bought a couple nice suits and a pair of good-quality shoes. I started going out for drinks and dinner sometimes with friends and colleagues. I had enough time to join a competitive soccer team and regularly make it to practices and games. Those were great days.

In addition to spending my new salary on things I wanted and needed, I also laid out a plan to start repaying the more than fifty thousand dollars in student debt I'd accumulated. After four years of living in rented rooms and tiny studio apartments, eating almost exclusively at the university's dining hall, and owning little more than a shelf of books and one suitcase of clothes, I finally had some stability in my life.

At Carrier, new engineering recruits spent a few months in each of several engineering operations within the company. I would have exposure to the reliability, software, electronic controls, and development groups. The projects I enjoyed most were those that combined both theory and practical application. Having a theory and making sure it played out in practice was fulfilling work and made me feel that what I was doing would eventually have a real-world impact.

I was acutely aware that my existing knowledge was insufficient for the program. Each time my assignment rotated, I went to my bookshelf—or trekked back to the Syracuse library—to find texts that could help me fill in the gaps between what I'd already learned and what I might need to know to do the job at hand. My biggest fear was getting caught as the engineer who didn't really know his stuff, so I avoided it by constantly researching and reading as if I were still a student. If I heard something I didn't understand during the day, at night I'd turn to my handbook of electrical engineering or another resource to bring myself up to speed.

There were two groups of people I learned a lot from during this time. The first were my fellow engineers, who taught by both good and bad example. I was surprised to see that the brightest engineers in the classroom were not necessarily the most successful in the workplace. I had a classmate who was hired at the same time I was. He'd been a 4.0 student. I thought he'd be the standout in the rotational program, but it was only a matter of weeks before project leaders started to complain about him not being a team player. It was shocking to see one of my peers who seemed so clearly destined for achievement struggling at the outset. The most successful engineers seemed to be the ones who were outgoing and cooperative; the ones who were able to connect with just about anyone in a matter of minutes; the ones who were eager to share ideas and collaborate.

The problem was, those exemplary coworkers were the opposite of me—a guy who'd sat in the back of every classroom and avoided talking to strangers whenever I could. After a lifetime of careful and sometimes awkward encounters brought about by my stutter or the challenges of speaking (and being understood) with my heavy accent, I had never been outgoing or effusive a day in my life. I envied some of my coworkers' ease when they spoke in a group or met someone new. I'd envied people like them before, but this experience was different. I was tired of feeling that way. I was ready to take steps to master the social skills I lacked.

The second group I learned a lot from was workers who had the practical experience to know how things worked. Some of these people were my project leaders and mentors in the engineering department, but not all of them had degrees in engineering. As part of my rotation, I worked with a lab technician who'd been with the company for decades. He was a grouchy, middle-aged guy who resisted the new product testing we had to do together. I thought his reluctance was telling me something about his attitude, but as it turned out, it was telling me something about his knowledge. He knew what would work and what would not. He knew his lab and the company's products better than anyone. He knew how to build and test a model and how to create the right conditions for an accurate assessment. And when he said a new idea was not going to work, he knew what he was talking about.

Of course, the tests still went on, and there was still knowledge to be gained from them. A couple of the other engineers were openly condescending to the tech and didn't see his value to the program, but I respected his experience. For four years I'd been the guy mopping floors, washing cars, walking security rounds, and filing papers. I knew that none of those jobs reflected my capabilities, and I swore I'd never underestimate anyone else because of his or her job. I paid attention and learned as much from that lab tech's experience as I learned from many of my engineering mentors.

Even as a new participant in the rotation program, I needed to be able to discuss the business components of my projects, and I became increasingly aware that I had no clue what I was talking about in that area. This side of the operation was something I wasn't able to brush up on with my textbooks. With a great job that ended at five every day, I had the time and the means to continue my education, so I decided to go back to school. I enrolled in Syracuse's engineering management master's program and started taking night classes that focused on subjects like finance and accounting. I chose classes around my work schedule, taking months off from school when I worked rotations in Indiana and Texas. It took a little less than two years to earn my master's degree.

At Carrier, one of my first assignments was in reliability engineering. We were investigating product failure rates, which typically follow what's called a "bathtub curve" pattern—the failure rate is high in the beginning, then falls and remains constant for a long period of time, and finally picks up again due to wear-out failures. My goal was to improve the product to mitigate its early failure rate, working toward a graph that looked more like a hockey stick—low and flat in the beginning and eventually curving upward as a machine ages. My job was to identify early failure causes and eliminate them. So I tested air conditioner blower motors, building a reliability test stand and running the machine exhaustively while monitoring its function. This was a project that was explained to me conceptually, but then I had to go build something original, do the testing, and eliminate the causes of failure. It was hands-on work that interested me. There were a bunch of early failure causes, like overheating and high-frequency noise, and I was able to work with the motor supplier to eliminate them.

One of the most interesting outcomes of my work at Carrier was getting my name on my first patent. I worked on a project team of four engineers to create a refrigerant control system. We designed an electronic control system with variable configurations that could be adjusted depending on the kind of refrigerant being recovered. All four of us were named on the patent.

Despite my firm footing in a professional track, there were challenges during this time, and one of these was my discovery that being a black man on a university campus and being black in a lot of other kinds of communities are two very different experiences. Most colleges take great pains to create atmospheres of cultural diversity and ethnic tolerance, and as a student at Syracuse, I had never experienced overt racism. During my time at Carrier, though, one of the components of my engineering rotation was a four-month stint in Huntington, Indiana. My experience on campus had done nothing to prepare me for the way I'd be treated there.

I flew out to start my assignment and set up an appointment to find an executive apartment with a relocation agent. She picked me up and told me she'd lined up half a dozen apartments for me to view. On paper, the first apartment looked promising—a two-bedroom in an upscale area near a few restaurants and a big park with soccer fields. When we got there and walked to the office to meet the manager, though, he greeted the two of us coolly and told my agent the apartment was no longer available. At the next apartment, we went on a walkthrough with a manager, who seemed polite but far from enthusiastic about renting the place—and by the time we got to the car he was calling my agent to tell her the place had been rented. At the third listing, we were again turned away without even seeing the apartment. It was the same at the fourth.

In the car, my agent shook her head. "I can't believe they're all rented," she said. "I spoke with all of them yesterday."

I guess I should have suspected what was going on, but I was naïve, so even though I was discouraged with how badly the search was going, it didn't cross my mind that I might be being deliberately blocked from these places. We stopped for gas, and I struck up a conversation with the woman at the next pump. I told her I was moving from Syracuse with Carrier and looking to rent in a nice apartment complex. I asked her if there was any other location she'd recommend we try.

The woman stared straight at me for a minute, and then she said, "I'm so sorry." She turned toward my agent and said, "You should know better. Nobody in this town is going to rent to him."

I was stunned. Nobody is going to rent to *him*? This wasn't the 1950s, when the KKK openly marched in Huntington, or the era of civil rights clashes in the 1960s. This was 1993, and discrimination of the kind this woman was suggesting seemed impossible—and was definitely illegal. I asked my realtor if all the fruitless showings had been because of my race.

"I'm very sorry, Mr. Edozien," she said, "but it's probably true. I know you'd like to stay in Huntington, but I think we might have better luck viewing properties in a neighboring city."

I got in the car and asked her to take me back to the plant. I stared out the window as I replayed our encounters with the apartment managers. Back at the plant, I told the director about the experience. He didn't have much to say on the subject except to agree that things might go easier for me somewhere nearby, suggesting Fort Wayne.

At the hotel that evening, I was still trying to process what had happened. I had two college degrees, a great job, good manners, strong references, and an agent from a reputable realty office—and

Huntington didn't want me. I would have been an ideal tenant, but none of my qualifications meant anything to the people holding the keys to those apartments. I'd been angry all afternoon, but back in my room, I was just profoundly sad that they were unwilling or unable to see anything about me beyond the color of my skin.

The next day I rented an executive apartment in Fort Wayne and turned my attention to the work that needed to be done at the plant. I didn't want to fight, and I didn't want to sulk. No town that didn't want me around was going to hold me back.

In the decades I've lived in the United States since this incident, I've seen and experienced racism in many forms, but during those first years after college, I was blind to how pervasive and sometimes subtle it can be. If I'd grown up experiencing the tensions and hostilities of racial division every day, I might have been less focused on factors like commute time and crime statistics and sought a rental in a more diverse community rather than choosing an insular, overwhelmingly white area. Or perhaps I would have keyed in on what was happening to me at the first property and confronted the manager. Maybe I would have internalized the rejection based solely on the color of my skin, letting it degrade my confidence or fester in the form of anger. Instead of doing any of those things, I was naïve and optimistic enough to be able to chalk the experience up as an anomaly. I acknowledged it, accepted it, and put it behind me. I continued to see a world of opportunity ahead of me.

Over the years, I have come to know far too many African American men and women who have lost—or who never had—confidence in opportunity. Their experiences have made them accustomed to a world of barriers. I often reflect on the fact that I was actually blessed to be largely oblivious to those barriers in the early years of my career. There was value in my being naïve. With no expectation of being treated with discrimination, I was able to throw myself wholeheartedly into every endeavor. I expected to be treated fairly—and most of the time I was.

––––––––––

That same year, hoping to make peace with my father, I traveled back to Nigeria for the first time since running away from home. I wrote to tell him I was coming but received no answer. The day I arrived, I asked to see him. He refused. I was hurt, but not surprised. My father is a proud man, and I had defied him. In Nigerian culture, that is rarely done—and never without consequences. The next day I went to his house. The servant who answered the door told me to wait, so I spent the day in a hard-backed chair, unacknowledged. The third day, I thought of a better way. I went back to the house with one of my cousins—a favorite of my father's and a good friend to me. I hoped that by then he'd feel he'd rejected me over my failures for long enough. My cousin and I waited together, and when he was finally called to see my dad, I was allowed to follow. My father focused intently on my cousin, refusing to look at me. I was not surprised at this ploy. It was a kind of grandstanding, a way to show my cousin—and the rest of the family—that I would not be easily accepted back into the fold.

Finally, on the fourth day, I was ushered in to see my father and he acknowledged me. His anger was palpable as he turned the conversation to my mother and his resentment toward her. I was willing to endure his admonishments about my behavior, but that was a line I would not cross, and I told him so. I said I'd come to talk with him about the relationship between us, not between him and my mother. I told him about my service in the army, my graduation with two degrees from Syracuse, and my accreditation as an engineer. By the time I left, he had stopped blatantly displaying anger and derision. He even seemed a little proud. It was enough for me to feel I had made my peace.

Back in Syracuse after my Indiana rotation, I had a meeting with a guy from the commercial side of the Carrier campus. At the time, my peers and I referred to everyone from that area as being "in marketing." We had very little concept of what it was they actually did over there. When I arrived, I was greeted by a young black man in an impeccably cut suit. Like me, he spoke with an accent. Unlike me, he exuded confidence. He introduced himself as Mark Taylor. He walked me through his building, which was completely unlike the engineering building I worked in. This was the place that visitors toured. It had soaring ceilings, dramatic lighting, and original art. After our meeting, Mark invited me to join him for lunch in the executive dining room—a nice change from the engineering cafeteria where I usually ate. We shared stories about our upbringings and educations. It turned out he was an engineer, too, but he also had an MBA. This guy had swagger and ambition, and he made no secret of his endgame: he wanted to be a CEO one day.

"You can't get to the top from the engineering lab," Mark declared. "Engineers make parts, but they don't make decisions."

To my ears, that was a revolutionary statement. I'd been all engineering, all the time since I'd arrived in New York. As a student, I'd always thought of every other course of study as a vague liberal art. Though I hadn't given it much thought, I held similar views about all the nonengineering departments in the company. I had no idea what all the people in those other buildings did, but I took it on faith that it all revolved around what we were doing in engineering.

Sitting in the executive dining room and talking with a man who had earned the same degree I'd earned and decided it wasn't enough to propel him toward his goals pulled me up short. He was basically telling me that my job was just making parts for his deals. I was a little offended and a little fascinated. But Mark wasn't trying to offend. He was friendly and full of interesting observations and thoughtful advice.

At the end of our lunch that day, I thanked him for his time. He suggested we get together again in a few days. That night, I replayed our conversation in my head. I wanted to be a decision-maker. That held more appeal for me than any other aspect of my work. I also wanted to achieve financial independence. On a sheet of paper, I calculated my salary and the raises I could expect to earn. I figured it would take me many years to reach a six-figure salary. I wanted to earn more, and, more importantly, I wanted to *do* more.

I started to get together with Mark regularly for lunches, and in the weeks and months that followed that first meeting, we became friends. I studied the way he carried himself, trying to figure it out. He walked with strength. He spoke with assurance. I'd never met anyone in America who shared my ethnicity and my "otherness" but also had that kind of confidence. I tried to learn from it and emulate it, but I also tried to duck the one piece of advice he repeatedly offered: that I needed to go back to school again and earn an MBA.

Why would I do that? I finally had a great job, a nice place to live, the opportunity to date pretty, educated girls—and here was this man I keenly admired telling me to give it up and go back to school. I was just wrapping up my engineering master's as a part-time student, but taking his advice would mean a bigger commitment: Quitting my job. Taking more loans. Moving somewhere new—something that worried me more after my experience in Indiana than ever before. Syracuse was comfortable for me, and I was doing well in my job. I was in no rush to leave.

In the end, though, my new friend's advice rang true. It was humbling to have the shortcomings of the objectives I'd focused on for so long held up to the light. I'd always thought that the engineers—and only the engineers—were the smartest guys in the room. Now I was beginning to see that intellect—and authority—come in many different forms. Mark Taylor had become a powerful influencer through an entirely different career path, and at the end of the day, everything I was doing in my department was at the behest of guys like him. I craved the opportunity to steer the work—not just to do it. I'd always wanted to *make* things. Now I realized that I also wanted to make things *happen*.

Early in the summer of 1994, I started applying to grad schools with MBA programs for the 1995–96 school year. I viewed the move as an investment in my professional future, and I was mindful of both the costs and the potential returns as I vetted programs. Because I was unwilling to take on another $100,000 in student debt without full confidence in the return on my investment, I focused on schools that had either the cachet to help ensure me a good placement after completing my degree or one-year programs that would let me accomplish it quickly. My highest-rated prospects had both.

The first application I completed was for the Katz School of Business at the University of Pittsburgh. They had a highly ranked, one-year MBA program. Just days after I submitted my application and GMAT, they called me. The admissions officer wanted to know which year I was applying for. I explained that I was applying for the fall of 1995, as was indicated on my application. She said there were still a few openings for the fall of 1994 and wanted to know if I'd be interested.

"I'd love to come this year," I told her, "but I haven't saved any tuition yet. I'm going to earn it between now and next summer."

Her next words would change the course of my future. She said, "What if we offered you a full scholarship?"

I didn't really believe it until I received the fax with my admissions offer, but there it was: 100 percent tuition and a stipend to use toward housing expenses.

I had just started a new project at Carrier, and I went back to my desk after receiving the fax to think about the implications of making this choice. My job was secure. I was treated well and respected at my company. I was learning every day from my peers and mentors. I'd thought I'd have a year to weigh my options for grad school— including the essential question of whether or not to go. Despite my best-laid plans, I knew better than to pass up this chance. When I spoke to Mark Taylor, he concurred, saying, "Carpe diem, Victor!"

I felt sick going down the hall to tell my project leader that I would be leaving his team. He had even written a recommendation for my MBA application when we'd both believed it was for a program that wouldn't start for more than a year. I worried he'd think less of me for abandoning my job. In his office, I showed him the letter and said, "Tom, I don't want to be ungrateful, but Pitt has offered me a spot for this year—and a full ride."

He glanced over my paperwork, shook my hand and told me that kind of offer just doesn't happen. He said, "Victor, you have to go."

Two weeks later I paid off the remaining month on my lease, moved out of my townhouse, and was on my way to Pittsburg. I'd be starting six weeks early to get a couple summer courses out of the way.

As our class took shape, it became clear that race had played a role in my admission. There were over 200 people in the program, and less than ten of us were black. I didn't know how to feel about that, but I did know that I had no choice but to excel in the program.

LESSON I LEARNED
Rise Above Bad Breaks

The idea that life isn't fair is true in all things, but it's especially evident in race relations. Within the span of a single year, I experienced two extremes in the way I was treated. My trip to Indiana was my first experience with the kind of insidious racism that keeps minorities out of communities that don't want us. Months later, I was not only welcomed but granted a full scholarship by a university that was working incredibly hard to include minorities. I had met all their standards in terms of grades and test scores and experience, but I hadn't just been accepted. They had reached out to me, invited me, and provided me with everything I needed to be able to attend.

No matter how you feel about affirmative action, you owe it to yourself to make the most of the opportunities that come your way. This is especially true for entrepreneurs. Sometimes your chances will be less than you'd like, or your opportunities narrower. Sometimes they will be more and broader than you dared to hope. You can't control that side of the equation. What you can control is what you do with your chance.

In all my dealings, but never more than when I entered the MBA program at Pitt, I know that my actions represent more than myself. I represent men, blacks, businessmen, fathers, soldiers, and my fellow Americans. The need I feel to excel is never just about personal success. It's also about the people who advocated for me and, to a lesser extent, those who stood in my way. And it's about those who will follow in my footsteps.

If someone passes you over because of your race, don't wallow in that rejection. There are other ways. And if someone gives you a chance, take it, and make sure you do your part to keep that avenue of opportunity open for the next person to travel. This attitude will help you develop a value-creating mind-set—a critical component in becoming the kind of entrepreneur who creates long-lasting impact and change.

Chapter 6

DRIVEN

*A dream doesn't become a reality through magic; it
takes sweat, determination, and hard work.*

—Colin Powell

Going to school without having to figure out where my tuition was coming from was the greatest academic experience of my life. For the first time, I was able to achieve my full potential as a student. In my first week at Pitt, a professor defined *mastery* as the confidence you feel when you approach a problem and know you can come up with a solution. I felt like I was well on my way to that goal as I studied economics, financial engineering, marketing, and a wide range of topics that fit my concentrations in finance and operations. By the time I finished the eleven-month program, I was no longer an insecure engineer trying to stay on top of the tasks at hand. I had found my confidence.

At the time, two of the most respected corporate finance development programs in the country for new MBA grads were at Ford and PepsiCo. They were considered training grounds for future Fortune 500 CFOs. When I was offered a position in the Ford program, I didn't hesitate to accept. I was honored to be considered, and I was intrigued by manufacturing in general and the auto industry in particular. I moved to Michigan to start my new job, eager to learn the corporate finance ropes with such a respected company.

It should have been an ideal position for me. I had an influential role. I was earning a great salary. I had opportunities to travel around the United States and Europe. In many ways, I'd achieved everything I thought I wanted in a career. And yet, the more familiar I became with the work, the more there was an emptiness about it that bothered me.

A big part of my job was preparing plant operation performance reports for my division president. I'd compile data on how the plant ran for a month and then analyze that data to come up with results and recommendations. It didn't take long to recognize that the plant I was analyzing wasn't making money; in fact, the division wasn't making money, either. Worse, the structure and culture of the operation were so rigidly determined that it was nearly impossible to make changes. I was documenting a failing operation, but it seemed I was in no position to improve it.

Another facet of my job was analyzing new program proposals. This should have been rewarding work, but the first time I took on one of these assignments, my in-depth analysis indicated that the program was going to be a dog. I could see no path to profitability. I took my report to the program manager with a recommendation against proceeding and a list of proposed changes for if it went forward. I thought I'd contributed something valuable—a peek into the future and a chance to revamp or scrap a doomed program.

Instead, I was directed to tweak my assumptions and analysis to make the project look better. It seemed that a true analysis wasn't wanted. Instead, my management was looking for a stamp of approval on something that was clearly going to tank in the long run. The "long-term" goal for some of these managers—though definitely not the company as a whole—was to get their projects going at any cost, knowing they'd be gone before the work proved ineffective.

This was not the career I went to business school for. I wanted to drive decisions, but my work was an exercise in futility. I had no interest in staying in the role of stymied analyst, and I started looking into the possibility of moving into private equity—a field where I'd have more independence and influence. I wasn't ready to make the leap to entrepreneurship yet, but I was circling closer to it.

Through a mutual contact, I learned about a boutique strategy consulting practice called the Lucas Group in Boston. The company's founder, Jay Lucas, had been a partner at Bain & Company, one of the world's largest strategy consulting firms and one of management consulting's most prestigious employers. His company was an innovative and respected player. Even though most of his analysts were straight out of Ivy League MBA programs, Jay was intrigued by my educational background and my engineering and industry experience. He flew me to Boston for an interview, and this time I knew well enough to make it clear that my professional goal was to work in a field where I could be a change-maker. I didn't want to analyze programs that were going to move ahead no matter what. Jay had no interest in presentation-driven consulting. Instead, his firm was pragmatic, analysis-based, and above all, results-driven. The firm was designed to analyze and drive investment decisions, then operating decisions, and then to stand by its clients.

"Your decisions will have impacts," Jay assured me, "immediate, short-term, and long-term." He said exactly the things I'd hoped to hear, and within days I'd accepted a position with his company.

I walked into the Lucas Group on my first day as the only African American man in the office and as one of the only individuals there coming from industry rather than from the Ivy League. Jay had gone to Yale, then Oxford, then Harvard. I was surrounded by entry-level consultants with impeccable pedigrees. The guy I shared a cube with was hired out of the MBA program at Dartmouth. He hadn't taken on a dime of debt and quickly let it slip that he was earning $25,000 more a year than I was. On Monday mornings, he'd come in talking about how he'd sailed his father's yacht from Providence out to Martha's Vineyard.

At times, the stories of his exploits transported me back to my days as a boy lounging at the Ikoyi Yacht Club in Lagos, but it felt like that experience had been a lifetime ago. For better or worse, I had grown up to be a different person than the one that boy might have become if he'd stayed in Nigeria. I had struggled and scraped and worked until my mind and body were so tired I could barely function to achieve the success I had in America. The idea of going back to any kind of reliance on my father, even if it meant a debt-free education or weekend trips to Nantucket, was impossible.

Despite the privilege of some of their upbringings, everyone at the Lucas Group earned his or her place every single day. This was during the heyday of investment analysis, and the industry in general—and prestigious firms like Lucas in particular—were almost Darwinian in their operations. They were composed of top people who were devoted to their work, and everyone in the group was hypercompetitive. I was working with the smartest, most intense people I'd ever met, just trying to hold my own. It was like being given a walk-on tryout for a professional sports team. Jay Lucas had given me a shot, but I had no idea whether I had what it would take to become part of the team. I made the cut, but I knew I'd have to continue to prove myself and earn my place every day.

As a result of both the caliber of the employees and the intensity of our commitment, we were doing incredible work—often from early morning until midnight or later. I had a new confidence since earning my MBA, but this was an environment where I felt the assumption was that I was not up to par unless I could prove differently.

Still, Jay Lucas had given me a shot, and once I was in his office, he took the time to teach me the ins and outs of the industry. He shared a world of wisdom about understanding strategy and about creating economic value. One of his most important tenets was to always focus on the growth side of a business rather than the costs. He encouraged me to look not just at the obvious possibilities but also for potential "white space"—as-yet unrecognized or unexploited potential for growth—and areas he called "competition-free zones." He expected his team to utilize all the traditional tools available to us to gather our data and complete our analyses, but he also pushed us to think outside the box and question existing mental models— to find or access or interpret information in ways that, perhaps, no other consultant had done yet.

As the junior guy, I threw myself into my first solo project as if my life depended on it. The client was a consumer confectionary company, and its VP of global sourcing wanted a benchmark of his competitors to understand what they were doing and how it differed from what he was doing. From that data, he hoped to discover ways to reduce his company's costs.

I worked fourteen- and sixteen-hour days doing my research. There was an ocean of material to uncover and understand, and I had to quickly figure out a system that would allow me to process everything into useful information. I spent time on-site with the client, combing through their competitive data, and then turned my attention to calling different companies and reviewing every shred of primary and secondary data available. In a study of that kind, you're not looking for a single answer. You're looking for a number of possibilities that are borne out by the concrete information on hand.

The catch was that even though the data was concrete, it was nearly impossible for the analysis to be equally solid. I was coming from an engineering background and a big corporation where everyone at all levels of management was risk-averse. In that environment, you needed to know you were right before you said a word. But in strategy consulting, there is an unavoidable level of ambiguity. You have to accept a certain amount of risk and ambiguity to function. I found that rather than working left to right—that is, following every bit of data or potential action item to its logical conclusion—I could work more effectively if I developed a number of hypotheses and worked them backward. I could quickly prove or disprove each one, leaving me with more time to explore all the possibilities. It was a fascinating and invigorating way to work.

I strove to nail down every fact and real number I could and then made the leap to an analysis based on what I knew. After six weeks of nearly round-the-clock work, I presented a summary, including a slew of detailed information about the client's competitors' operations, and a list of actionable insights—steps I recommended the client take in the short and long term. When I was finished, I left the room and waited to hear whether I'd adequately represented the venerable Lucas Group, or if the executives had seen through the recruit who hadn't come from Harvard, who struggled to minimize his accent and quell his stutter, who was earning 20 percent less than his weekend-yachting officemate—maybe for good reason.

As it turned out, my analysis held up fine. The client said I knocked it out of the park and immediately began implementing the strategies I'd proposed. He even sent a letter to my management requesting that I be on his team for all future consulting.

That was the assignment that gave me credibility in the office and allowed me to hold my head higher as I met new clients. Almost overnight, I went from feeling like an outsider to feeling like a respected member of the team. It didn't take long for me to close the earning gap between me and my officemate, either.

LESSON I LEARNED
Create More Value than You Cost

My time at the Lucas Group taught me that one of the most critical facets of entrepreneurship is simply putting in the hard work and the hours. There is always competition, and you have to know that someone else is out there every single day, trying to eat your lunch. If you want to prevail, you need to work harder and smarter, and be more innovative and creative, than that competitor. The nature of consultancy in general and of the Lucas Group in particular was vigorously competitive, with my peers and me vying with one another, with other consultancies, and for any competitive edge we could grant our clients. There were times when this work was inspired, but just as often it was simply a matter of grinding away at what had to be accomplished, working long hours at maximum effort. And we did it all with never-let-them-see-you-sweat attitudes, wanting our work to look effortless even when we were mentally and physically drained.

There is a saying I've often reflected on both as an employee and as an entrepreneur: create more value than you cost. Whether I'm questioning my own productivity or fielding a request from an employee for a raise, I always come back to value. If you're creating it, any failure on your part to show up or deliver will be painfully obvious. If you're not, then things will go on just the same without you.

If you want to foster your entrepreneurial spirit, get in the habit of delivering a high level of performance in everything you do. Focus on creating value. Whether you're functioning as an employee or an entrepreneur, your input, ideas, and labor should be indispensable. If you can do that, you'll make yourself a strong and invaluable competitor.

Chapter 7

CRISIS OF CONSCIENCE

The one thing that doesn't abide by majority rule is a person's conscience.

—Harper Lee

n the fall of 1997 and spring of 1998, two unrelated events led to a change in my priorities and, ultimately, in the trajectory of my career. The first of these was an assignment through the Lucas Group to analyze the financial performance of a Louisiana-based grocery chain. The second was a brutal takedown in a regional league soccer game that literally knocked me off my feet—and left me that way for months.

I went to New Orleans in the fall of 1997 to help analyze the assets, sales, and productivity of a recently bought-out grocery chain for its new owners. The Schwegmann chain wasn't just any business to Louisiana locals. It was a part of the New Orleans community and culture, an entity tightly tied to the region's beloved cuisine. People grew up with memories of their local Schwegmann as the place where they bought their grocery staples, locally made king cakes and regional specialties, and everything from sporting goods and gardening equipment to records and clothes. The stores were the first supermarkets in the South, and at one time a Schwegmann outpost was reputed to be the biggest supermarket in the world. The chain was also a major economic force, employing more than 5,000 people.

By the time I checked into my French Quarter hotel to start my analysis of Schwegmann assets and operations, I'd been working for the Lucas Group for two years. I'd proven my effectiveness at this kind of job, and I was proud of my accomplishments. I was holding my own in an office with a very rarified workforce.

On that first morning, I pressed my suit, walked through the opulent lobby, and stood below the wrought-iron balconies, waiting for my car. From there, I drove out to the first market on my list to meet the manager and go over the books. I would spend several weeks shaking the hands of managers, poring over store records, and meeting Schwegmann employees along the way. As I strayed further away from my base on Bourbon Street, the neighborhoods got poorer, and it was impossible not to notice that in this southern city, poverty was closely intertwined with race. Almost all of the employees and the shoppers in the poorest neighborhoods I visited were black, like me. I'd never been anywhere before where entire communities were so clearly stratified not just by income but also by race.

Schwegmann had become mired in debt, and its operations were too expensive. There was a glaring need to cut overhead and reduce the workforce. Acknowledging facts like those is part of the reality of advising and consulting for private equity clients, and I'd done the same type of work before. But the fate of the stores in those New Orleans neighborhoods weighed on me. I knew there would be ripples throughout the grocery chain and the communities it served because of my analysis. I couldn't help but question who I should be aligned with, and during those days, I had a sinking feeling that maybe I was identifying with the wrong side.

When I dug into the books, one of the biggest problems in the poorest neighborhoods was high "shrink." The term refers to the discrepancy between the book inventory and actual stock at a given location. In the grocery industry, shrink can be attributed to a number of factors, including things like spoilage, inventory errors, and shoplifting. Shoplifting was a big issue in some of these stores. It was so prominent that at times it would even happen while I was on-site. I'll never forget the mid-November day when a man walked into the location I was analyzing, tucked a big frozen turkey under each arm, and took off running out of the store, down the street, and out of sight. That kind of shrink is hard to fix. The security guard ran a half a block behind him, but that was it. No store guard earning minimum wage is going to—or should—risk life and limb to take down a turkey thief.

The fiscal realities of the stores were discouraging. Some locations had no path to profitability and would have to be shuttered. To cut costs, there would have to be layoffs at other stores as well. The thought of having a hand in taking jobs out of these struggling communities was hard for me to accept. I checked and rechecked my data, hoping to find a way to turn the stores around rather than shutting them down. I had a lot of time to think about it at the end of each day as I went back to my four-star hotel—a place that seemed to exist in an entirely different New Orleans from the one where I spent my working hours.

Near the end of the analysis period, in mid-December, I got on a conference call with the executives who were orchestrating the restructuring of the Schwegmann chain and their bankers in New York. I laid out my recommendations, including turnaround plans for some locations and recommendations to close others. Both scenarios included layoffs, which weighed on my conscience. I'd been in the stores every day, shaking hands with the workers, asking them questions, and assessing each operation. They were much more than the numbers that represented them on my spreadsheets. In my plan, the layoffs would be implemented in January.

My analysis was met with general approval, but one of the bankers had a logistical question. He asked why the layoffs were slated for January rather than effective immediately. It had not occurred to me that the new owners might lay off a slew of workers with no warning just two weeks before the holidays, and I said so. The banker's tone changed from curious to chastising.

"There are interest payments due, Victor," he said. "Do you think those obligations can be deferred until January?"

That was the day I started thinking a lot about profit—not just about how desirable it was and how to attain it but also about whether it should be maximized at any cost. Money has to be made. We all know that. But people can't be excluded from profit calculations. Without them, it's just empty math that forgets the real reason for economy and industry. I was beginning to realize a fundamental difference between what I wanted to do with my life and the function I was performing.

I began to believe, not just in theory but in a practical and analytical way, that it had to be possible to find a balance between the way I made money and the way it affected people's lives. I had wanted to be a change-maker, yes, but I wanted my changes to have a positive impact.

I spent a lot of time in the months that followed my assignment in New Orleans considering my options and wondering what I could do to have an impact I could feel good about. Time and again I came to the conclusion that I should follow through in the most obvious way—by buying a company and running it in a way that respected both people and profits. But I did not have the kind of cash that would be required to buy a company, and I had no idea where to start.

––––––––––

Over the years, I've often explained my attraction to the Lucas Group and the work we did there in terms of soccer. When I lived in Syracuse, I'd worked my way up through pickup games and local leagues until I earned a spot in a semi-pro league. Everyone on my team had another vocation, but when we came together, we were deeply dedicated—practicing, traveling, and playing our hearts out to the point of leaving blood, sweat, and tears on the field. Working at Ford had been like being back in a pickup league, playing games in which nothing was at stake. Players came and went, and it was clear they were engaged in a pastime, not fulfilling a mission. The Lucas Group, however, put me back on a competitive field. We were a team. We worked ourselves to the bone. We were determined to win.

Given that analogy, it's rather ironic that the second event that led to my exiting the Lucas Group and striking out on my own was a soccer game. I lived in Lexington and played in a regional amateur league, and one night in May, 1998, we were pitted against a team from Boston's south side on their home field. It was a beautiful, clear evening, and I was having a great game until I was hit by a merciless backsliding tackle. The guy had my cleats between his legs as he took me down, and as he wrenched me over, he broke my knee and my ankle. I heard the bones crunch, knew I wasn't going to walk off that field, and started screaming. I'd never experienced pain like that. My teammates lifted me up and carried me to the sidelines. I looked down at my gruesomely dangling leg and swallowed the urge to vomit. One teammate drove me to Beth Israel Hospital, and a second drove my car home. In the emergency room, I was swooped into a back area where a nurse cut my clothes off and a surgeon explained that I'd had a complicated break that needed to be operated on immediately. I remember nodding and signing a stack of paperwork giving permission for the surgery. After that, I was finally, mercifully, given pain medication.

When I got my cast off and started physical therapy, I was distraught to discover that I couldn't walk. This was more than the lingering effect of the injury or muscle atrophy. The therapist told me there was something fundamentally wrong with my leg, saying, "I'm not sure if I can get you back on your feet."

I went to an ankle specialist who asked me to step into the hall and demonstrate my gait as best I could. Another doctor came up beside him and I couldn't help but hear their hushed conversation. "My God," the specialist said as he stared at my leg. "They bolted it the wrong way."

The surgery after my accident had been done wrong, and unless I agreed to let the specialist re-break my ankle and repair it correctly, I would never walk again. *If* his work was successful, I'd need to follow up with a knee specialist about the possibility of further repair at the other end of the injury.

It took five different surgeries over a period of three years to fully repair my leg and get me back on my feet. During that entire period I was physically challenged, alternating between the use of crutches, a wheelchair, a cane, and a knee scooter. I went to physical therapy multiple times each week when I wasn't traveling for business. In the end, it wasn't any shortcoming of my work with the Lucas Group that was the final straw in my departure from the company; it was my own reticence to continue accepting a salary for a job I could not perform at 100 percent. Maybe it was a carryover from my years working menial jobs for low pay, or the fact that Jay Lucas had taken a chance on me and I didn't want to let him down. But I was unable to continue to accept a paycheck for work I wasn't able to fully complete. I needed to take some time to focus on my recovery and decided I'd reached the right moment to reassess my professional and personal priorities.

Something had to change for me to be at peace with my role in the business world, but before I could make a move, I needed to get my strength back.

LESSON I LEARNED
Have a Positive Impact

The most effective and successful entrepreneurs I know didn't check their convictions at the door. Rather, they established them early and found ways to align their personal and professional priorities. The Lucas Group gave me a chance to become a change-maker, fulfilling my desire to do work that had an impact. During my time with them, I got hooked on the business of private equity investments and consulting. The idea of digging into every detail of how a business is run and finding a way to make it work better and smarter was intoxicating, especially because our clients were quick to act on our recommendations. But as that phase of my career came to an end, I no longer wanted to work with profits as my only priority. I wanted to follow the same steps, but with an endgame of saving and creating good jobs along with earning profits. The people on the spreadsheets matter, and that fact was moving to the forefront of my entrepreneurial vision. It is a mental shift I have never regretted, and one that has benefited me in terms of both psychological dividends and monetary profit. It is important to define your convictions. Truly understand what matters to you, what you stand for, and why you do what you do.

Never forget that your decisions have impacts not just on profits, but also on people. Your most rewarding investments will likely be tied to choices that give priority to both.

Chapter 8

ASABA

You don't have to see the whole staircase. Just take the first step.

—Martin Luther King, Jr.

For a short time I lived off my savings, all the while wondering what my next step should be.

I thought perhaps I could make an investment in the international market. At the time, there was some privatization of government assets going on in Nigeria. There was a paper mill in the western part of the country slated to go to private industry, and the idea of buying it held a strong appeal for me. It was in my parents' homeland. If run well, it would employ 1,500 people in a remote area of the country that desperately needed jobs, and because there were no competitors in western Africa, it could be expected to be profitable. I knew I wanted to be a force for creating jobs, and I thought I could win the bid for the facility.

Unfortunately, during this period business with the government in Nigeria dealt heavily in corruption and bribes, and I was an outsider. I had an accent there, too, and was considered a foreigner. In the end, it didn't work out, and to this day, the mill remains dormant.

As my leg got stronger and I slowly got back on my feet, I kept coming back to my stint at Schwegmann in New Orleans and to another assignment I'd taken afterward, assessing a Phoenix supermarket chain that served a predominantly low-income Hispanic community. In analyzing yet another failing supermarket chain, I felt strongly that there must be a way to turn the stores around rather than shuttering them. It was easy to look at the population of potential shoppers and believe that, because they didn't have a high per-capita income, there was no market there. But I didn't see it that way.

The populations did not have high levels of disposable income, but they represented significant—and growing—income density. The people in New Orleans and Phoenix who were seeing their local supermarkets closing were still shopping somewhere—they still had fundamental retail needs and wants—but that demand was no longer being met by the firms I worked with. Someone needed to step in and offer products to these underserved communities, and I was fascinated with how they might make, market, and sell those products to this unusual buying demographic. The communities needed to be served. A business opportunity existed. There was potential in that equation for some kind of win/win endeavor that was being squandered.

Taking this to heart, I began to weigh the possibility of starting my own consulting group. When I spoke with Jay Lucas, he offered good advice, as always. He told me to concentrate on a single area—to find a niche to call my own. He also told me to choose an area that had a strong pull for me, something with an angle I could get behind that would work naturally.

What mattered to me was being a part of the creation of value, jobs, and job security. Ideally, I wanted to create all of those things for minority and underserved populations. With that germ of an idea, in 1999, I launched my own company, Asaba Group consulting practice. The name was a nod to my family heritage. Historically, the Edoziens have been a royal family of the city of Asaba in Nigeria. I'd come a long way to separate myself from my family history, but as time passed, I wanted to find a place for it and for my father in my life. My professional focus would be finding winning growth strategies for underserved populations in multicultural environments. I hoped to do it all in a culturally sensitive way.

As an auto industry veteran, it didn't take long for me to turn my interest to the supply-chain side of major businesses. For many reasons, companies and government entities want and need to have businesses owned by ethnic minorities in their supply chains. That choice is socially responsible, it's sometimes mandated by the government, and it gives companies a strong and organic connection to an increasingly powerful purchasing demographic. It can also lead to new business opportunities.

However, some companies and government agencies don't know how to effectively engage minority-owned businesses as new suppliers, and some suppliers don't know how to make the most of the opportunities available. The auto industry in particular is one where countless companies function based strictly on what has worked in the past, without looking to new information to stream-line, innovate, or respond to coming market changes. In my initial analysis, I encountered company after company led by someone who operated based on an *I've been doing it this way for twenty-five years* mental model, and many of those companies seemed to be headed for trouble.

I knew that companies in the private equity portfolios I'd seen were experiencing lower failure rates than those that were not being molded by current industry insights, and I thought it was time minor-ity-owned, supply-chain businesses started benefiting from the same kinds of analysis and insight their equity-driven competitors were receiving. I wanted to find a way to bring the same kind of creative spark and insight that was driving the most successful companies in the supply chain to the minority-owned supplier base. I believed that if I could leverage my private equity experience to offer industry and commodity insights, trend predictions, and strategy advising, I could help those companies improve their game. If I could offer this service in coordination with automakers—the forces that spend billions of dollars a year and dictate these markets—I could potentially help transform supply-chain businesses that were barely hanging on into securely profitable ones. The benefits of fostering healthy, efficient suppliers would extend up and down the industry.

I saw a need for greater expertise and for a liaison between cor-porations/government agencies and minority suppliers. I knew there were ways to make the most of opportunities, leverage government programs, and empower suppliers, all of which could create both jobs and consumers. I needed to figure out what was needed to boost this process and enhance these relationships.

At first, my little company wasn't much. I worked out of my basement. The biggest challenge in building my consulting business wasn't figuring out the best strategies for corporate and supplier success—I knew I had valuable insight to offer both sides—it was getting noticed by the industry. I had no means to share what I'd discovered. In short, I knew how to be an excellent consultant, but I didn't really understand yet how to be in the business of consulting—how to take what I'd learned and put it in the service of clients.

Once again I went back to my friends at the Lucas Group for guidance, and once again I got good advice. "One of the key things you need to learn, Victor," Jay Lucas told me, "is that it's not your technical skills that will carry you through. It's your ability to work with people and make connections." In other words, I had to acquire and hone business development skills. Despite all my years of education and experience in the industry, that was a whole new skill set.

Just as I'd always done, I started learning at the bookshelf. I read Ford Harding's *Rain Making,* Keith Ferrazzi's *Never Eat Alone,* and other books about building relationships and business contacts. I worked on my handshake, my small talk, my ability to control the direction of a conversation. I made a point of finding opportunities to meet new people and practice strategies to keep from getting nervous or letting my stutter betray me.

I also studied the ways other successful consultancies got on the map with their clients. I noticed that the consultancies I admired had built their reputations in part on their proprietary methods and intellectual thought pieces. A well-received white paper or an academic or industry book was the ultimate credential to make corporations sit up and take notice of a consultant. As I continued to research and better understand the field of supply chains, I knew I could produce a solid summary of the state of minority-owned supply-chain businesses, how their stake could be improved, and why that improvement would benefit corporate and government clients. But even if I wrote it, I lacked an avenue to get it into the hands of the right people.

It was around that time that I first met Courtland Cox. He had been appointed by President Clinton to serve as Director of the Minority Business Development Agency in Washington, D.C. If there was one man in a position to help me begin to make connections and do some good for minority business owners, he was the guy. I wrote him a letter and asked for a meeting. I told him about my auto industry experience, my time in private equity consulting, and my particular interest in industry supply-chain participation for minority-owned businesses.

To my amazement, he wrote back and invited me to come to Washington in January of 2000. I was terrified to go alone and enlisted two friends to come along and act as though they were a part of the Asaba Group team. I'd have an hour to explain how I could effect positive change for both minority-owned businesses and corporations. I lived and breathed my presentation for weeks before the meeting, gathering and analyzing data and fine-tuning my positions into five major topics:

1. **The state of the auto industry,** including data on market size, product categories, and supplier characteristics. I focused on trends I thought would be critical in the coming five years and the forces that were driving them.

2. **Growth opportunities,** including opportunities for automotive suppliers in general and specifically for minority suppliers. I zeroed in on how I believed the industry would

leverage their suppliers and what capabilities they would need to be successful.

3. **Automotive supplier opportunities,** including winning supplier strategies and which characteristics were defining emerging manufacturer/supplier relationships at different tiers.

4. **Investment considerations,** highlighting the economic reasons why investors should choose minority automotive suppliers, including examples of potential opportunities.

5. **A call to action** for current and future minority suppliers and an outline of the specific economic opportunities that existed for them.

Throughout my presentation, I emphasized that the role of minority-owned supply businesses had changed from when many of the major industry players began encouraging their involvement in the 1960s, 1970s, and 1980s. This was no longer just a decision of social conscience or local loyalty; now it was good business. One of the things some corporations had not yet considered or implemented in their long-range plans was the fact that nearly *90 percent* of growth in their entry-level buyer segment over the next several decades would be among minorities. I explained that building strong corporate links to minority communities through engagement with minority-owned supply businesses had the potential to build positive brand recognition in those communities, to enhance internal corporate diversity efforts, and to promote economic growth in communities full of future customers.

When I finished, Courtland thanked me for coming and offered me the opportunity I'd hoped for: he asked if I'd write a white paper for the auto industry and offered a grant to pay for it. If I could deliver a paper worthy of presentation to auto industry executives, financial investors, and minority suppliers, I would have the credential I needed most to build a successful consultancy. As my "colleagues" and I were leaving the office, Courtland shook my hand and said, "Next time, you don't need to bring your friends for moral support. I believe you can do this."

That meeting, and the publication of the paper I prepared in follow-up, was a game changer. The next time Courtland Cox held a gathering for people from the auto sector, he invited me to present my paper. Two executives from DaimlerChrysler approached me after my presentation. Tom Sidlik was Chrysler's Executive VP for Procurement and Supply, and Jethro Joseph was their Senior Manager for Supplier Diversity and Development. After posing a few questions about my research, they asked if I'd be willing to come to Detroit to share my presentation with their supplier diversity council. They would pay my travel expenses.

I just wanted to know where and when.

Weeks later, I was walking into Chrysler's vast technology center in Auburn Hills, Michigan. The 5.4 million-square-foot facility was the second largest building in America, behind only the Pentagon. I felt like a miniature version of myself as I crossed its threshold, lugging my materials in a shoulder bag and leaning heavily on my cane. Just getting in the door felt like a long trek, and I stopped to catch my breath before moving deeper into the building.

I gave my presentation to a room full of executives, and when I was finished, Tom announced he was going to launch a new program, the DaimlerChrysler Minority Enterprise Initiative. He informed the attendees that the Asaba Group would play a key role in the program. I hadn't expected the announcement or his recognition—neither had the incumbent suppliers who were in the room.

One of their representatives quickly interjected, saying that I could subcontract through her company. Tom seemed to anticipate this, and with a glance and a nod to Jethro across the room, he said, "No. Mr. Edozien will work directly with us."

Later in the day, the same woman pulled me aside and told me I'd be better off subcontracting through her company. "You don't have the necessary relationships to do this on your own," she told me. "And you haven't paid your dues."

In the long run, I would in fact have to sub through this company to work with other auto manufacturers, and it became a fraught process during which I would provide my best research and insight, and the supplier would scrub my name from it and pass it off as their own. But because the executive team at Chrysler believed in me, I never had to fight for recognition of my work with them. By the time I left the mammoth technical building that afternoon, I had agreed to the terms of my first industry consulting contract.

The Department of Commerce received enough positive feedback to my first white paper that Courtland contracted with me to research and write on eight additional topics, both inside and outside the auto industry. Those papers became the intellectual basis for much of the work I was able to do after.

The Asaba Group was on its way, and I was able to rent a real office and hire a small team to work with me. I no longer needed to impose on my friends to pretend they were employees to make my company look legitimate. As word got out about the group and the attention to detail and insight we brought to our work, we quickly reached the next level. At every step, I worked to cultivate good relationships, even friendships. In one of our earliest meetings, Courtland Cox had advised me to be ever mindful of making friends, not enemies. He phrased it in a way that was so blunt I'd never forget it. "You need people inside your tent peeing out, not outside your tent peeing in," he said. "You need people to know you and like you, Victor."

Using an adaptation of the model I'd prepared for Chrysler and later for other auto industry leaders, in 2003 I won a multimillion dollar contract with the US Air Force to provide technical and managerial assistance to small, local manufacturing businesses in its parts chain. I would advise them on growing their businesses and addressing capital issues they'd face as they grew. This project would ultimately allow me to work with close to one hundred different manufacturers and suppliers for the air force and to help each of them make the most of the opportunities they were given.

Within two years of founding Asaba, I was doing exactly what I'd dreamed of when I struck out on my own: using my talents to help create and maintain both profits *and* jobs. It was my first true taste of successful entrepreneurship, and it didn't take long for me to begin to think about the next step. I could have a positive impact in a limited capacity on the advisory side of the business, but in order to truly put my theories into practice and become a job creator, I'd need to own a business outright.

LESSON I LEARNED

When Your Opportunity Arrives, Deliver

There's a 2,000-year-old saying attributed to the Roman philosopher and politician Seneca that I'm always mindful of in my professional life: *"Luck is what happens when preparation meets opportunity."* The fact is, there is no one path to entrepreneurial success, but rather a long maze of choices and chances you take. Along that path, however, there will come a time—or many times, if you're fortunate—when you're given an opportunity. When it happens, be sure you deliver.

Courtland Cox gave me my first big chance as a consultant, and I left nothing on the table when I prepared and took that first presentation to Washington. Given the chance to write a white paper with the potential to reach the highest echelons of my target industry, I delivered one that was thorough and original. When Chrysler executives invited me to address their supply-chain companies, I reinvented my presentation for their focus and offered valuable insights into their future profitability. That effort earned my company a half-million-dollar contract to work with their suppliers. I re-engineered that same, successful model and pitched it to the government, eventually landing a five-year air force contract. Those steps—each one an opportunity that I had to deliver on—put my consultancy on the map.

Many would-be minority entrepreneurs tell me that a lack of financial resources is the reason they don't strike out on their own. I can tell you from my experience as an innovator and an investor that if you have an original and viable idea—and if you deliver when you're given an opportunity to do so—the capital will come. Someone will believe in you.

Chapter 9

MAKING THE LEAP

We live in a world where courage is in far shorter supply than genius.

—Peter Thiel

I n the fall of 2004, a business trip brought me to South Africa, where I found myself rolling and pitching over the waves on a ferry from Cape Town to Robben Island. It was the last day of a trip hosted by Chrysler to help American minority-owned supply companies foster relationships and partnerships with black-owned South African businesses. As an authority in the field and an ally in Chrysler's efforts to support its supply-chain companies, I'd been included on the guest list. Spending a week traversing South Africa's cities with a group of industry leaders was an amazing opportunity—

one that helped me establish connections that are still important more than a decade later.

Robben Island was my last excursion before heading home, and it was also the most meaningful. The island is the site of the prison where Nelson Mandela was incarcerated for eighteen years. I knew quite a bit about Mandela, but that day I learned that among the reasons Robben Island has long been used for isolation—as a prison, a leper colony, and an animal quarantine station—are the strong currents, high waves, and rocky coastline that create inhospitable boating conditions around it. As our ferry made its way, the seas tossed us up and down, side to side. More than once, we listed so far over I thought for sure we would capsize.

Sid Taylor, another Chrysler guest who owned a number of manufacturing plants and was one of my consulting clients, rolled with the swells beside me—both of us inexperienced with boating and terrified. When we finally arrived at the island, we put our fear and nausea aside and went to see the cell that held one of history's greatest political heroes for nearly two decades. It was hard to imagine how Mandela, who labored in a quarry every day, slept on a mat on the floor each night, and was isolated in every way from the world beyond the island, could have kept his wits in that cell, let alone matured into the intelligent, revered statesman he would one day become. It was a profound experience for me to see the place where his will outweighed every factor against him.

Sid and I braced ourselves for the ferry ride back to Cape Town. Both of us were silent and uncomplaining as the sea thrashed the boat on the return trip. When we reached land again, he shook my hand and asked me to come visit him at his home in Detroit one day soon. He said he had something important to discuss with me.

When I arrived at his house a few weeks later, Sid didn't waste any time getting to the point of the visit. Ever since that day on the ferry, he'd been thinking about mortality and legacy. He wanted to create a succession plan for his company, SET Enterprises. SET was the result of lifetime of labor, dedication, and sacrifices, and Sid wanted to ensure it would go on long after he stepped down from its helm. After working with me as a consultant and spending time with me in South Africa, he wanted me to be a part of his long-term plan. I was honored by his request but daunted by the proposal. He asked me to start by joining the SET board, but his long-term objective was for me to buy a majority interest in the company a few years down the line.

"You'll have to have resources and relationships to make it happen, Victor," he told me, "but I believe you're the right person to carry this company forward."

In order to comply with this request, I'd have to come up with a 50 percent stake and control of the board of this large corporation—a challenge I was willing to aspire to, but not one I could guarantee. Sid was positive and diplomatic, telling me that he trusted in my leadership ability and my resourcefulness to raise the funds. I left his house with a vision of one day taking the helm of the company. From my consulting engagements with SET, I was familiar with its financials and operating performance. SET was in the highly competitive steel processing sector. It wasn't going to be an easy transaction and would require a new strategy to ensure its long-term competitiveness.

———————

Back at my office in Massachusetts, I was working on a more concrete and immediate deal. I'd been spending much of my time preparing to take the next step in entrepreneurship—the biggest step. After years of analyzing and examining the auto supply chain from the outside, I was ready to become a part of it, to own a functioning, nuts-and-bolts piece of the industry that created and sustained both product and jobs.

In my work for Chrysler, I'd done a lot of supplier analysis and developed a good eye for what kinds of companies were profitable and which were likely to fail. I could pore over the data for any company and learn a lot about how it operated, whether it was positioned for success, and how it might fare as the industry moved forward. Of course, there are always unpredictable factors, but I could glean a lot of information from the available data.

During this process, a company called KenSa caught my eye. KenSa manufactured electrical wiring systems, and the company's actions indicated that it was almost entirely focused on lowering labor costs to ensure its profitability. In the early 2000s, its management shut down multiple operations in Michigan and shipped the work to Mexico. Before long, after finding cheaper labor in Honduras, they moved the jobs again. Eventually, much of the work would go to China for an even lower labor rate. When the company finally met its demise, it was after chasing labor costs all over the globe.

In 2004, only one KenSa factory remained in Michigan, a wiring harness plant in the small town of Harbor Beach. The factory seemed destined to follow in the footsteps of the company's other domestic facilities. Most of the workers had already been laid off. Of those who remained, some had been kept on staff so they could travel to Central America to train their replacements. Business was slow, morale was low, and there was an expectation in the community, as well as in the industry, that it was just a matter of time before the place was shuttered for good.

I have always believed—even before I bought my first plant—that relentlessly chasing labor costs is neither a useful nor an honorable strategy. There will always be someone who can get to a lower wage cost, so it's not an area in which I choose to stake my aspirations for any business. I wasn't going to buy a plant and turn it around by paying its workers less. I wanted to find a better path to sustainable profitability—one that recognized that a company has to invest in its people to be worthwhile.

Despite the discouraging outlook for the Harbor Beach facility, there were aspects of the operation that kept me circling back to its possibilities. Most of the KenSa operations that had already been sent across borders involved high-volume manufacturing—making thousands of the same part, day after day. This place was different. Harbor Beach did not produce high volumes. Instead, it kept up with low-volume orders for multiple part numbers, and most of those parts were built for immediate shipping to dealerships that would not be willing to wait more than a day or two for what they needed. Much of the business didn't support manufacturing; it supported service and repairs. As a result, the operation didn't lend itself to economies of scale. It was more about economies of scope: efficiencies gained from producing small batches of a variety of products.

I couldn't predict demand, but I knew that millions of end customers—drivers of more than 200 million cars on American roads—would not wait around for parts that had to ship from Mexico or Honduras or China. If I could focus the work more on meeting aftermarket demand and less on new car part production, this facility could become nimble and capable of rapid delivery to dealerships.

The more I thought about it, the more I believed I could make the business profitable. First, though, I'd have to figure out a way to buy it. I didn't have nearly enough money to purchase it outright, so I made a list of all the assets I could use and calculated what I'd need to borrow. My liquid assets amounted to about $300,000. After running all the numbers, I went to several institutions seeking a loan. I started with the big banks in Detroit: Bank of America, Chase, Comerica, and Fifth Third. At each one, I made an appointment and came in with a presentation about the factory and my vision for it. I changed out a couple slides in each presentation so it would feature the name of the bank I was visiting.

Most of them heard me out, but every one of them turned me down.

Next I decided to approach the regional banks with branches in Harbor Beach. I figured no business would stand to gain more from a turnaround of the KenSa factory than a local lender. There were three banks in town. The first two weren't interested in lending to me, but the branch manager of the last one—Chemical Bank—didn't exactly say no. Instead he told me his branch didn't make the kind of loan I was seeking, but that I could try the Caro, Michigan, branch. I made an appointment in Caro, another small town north of Detroit, to ask for my $1.5 million loan. It felt like a last chance. I was running out of banks.

The banker's name was Doug Herringshaw, and he welcomed me into his office. I did not see another black person during my entire time in the town or at the bank, but I wasn't going to be intimidated. I needed a substantial loan, and I was prepared to make my case for it just like the next guy. Plus, I was getting really good at giving my presentation after so much practice. Doug listened closely as I launched into my spiel about why the bank should trust me with its money. I had a PowerPoint full of charts and graphs, and I explained the necessity for this plant to employ a knowledgeable and agile workforce. I told him how I'd analyzed every shred of data available and that I was certain there was a path to profitability. I explained how, during my years consulting with the Lucas Group, we'd often found that people actually didn't *know* where they were making money and where they were losing it, but that I would determine which parts were currently profitable and eventually make them all profitable. I told him that both my engineering and strategy consulting backgrounds would see me through the process.

Finally, I explained that I was not interested in innovation or profitability alone. I wanted and needed to tie any personal and professional benefit from my investment to jobs and opportunities for the community. If I can't have both, I told him, I don't have the motivation to buy the plant. Historically, Harbor Beach's wiring harness plant had been a driver of the local economy. I wanted to make it one again. I felt like I was looking down a long road but could see my way clearly from beginning to end.

When I finished my presentation, Mr. Herringshaw flipped through the copy I'd given him. Then he got up, closed the door, and turned back to me. "Look, son," he said, "there's something about you and the way you're going about this. I believe in you, and I believe in what you're trying to do."

I held my breath.

"We're going to invest in you," he said. "You're going to get your loan."

I could hardly believe what I was hearing. I'd walked into the bank feeling I didn't have nearly enough capital, collateral, or experience to make the deal. I'd worried that my lack of personal and professional connections to the area would be my downfall. I'd been turned down by nearly a dozen other banks. But I was walking out with the funding to buy a manufacturing plant and absolute freedom to do my best to turn it around.

That sequence of events would never have happened to me in Nigeria or South Africa or China or even in England. It was a uniquely American moment, and it was one that would, in many ways, give me the opportunity to chart the course of my professional life from that day until this one. I walked out of the bank full of gratitude and patriotism.

I was close to having all the capital I needed—more than $1.7 million of the $2 million total. I went to the owner of KenSa, Hal Zaima, and asked if he'd hold the remaining balance in seller's debt and allow me to pay it off over the next five years. I was already going to be dealing with him, because all the management of inventory, shipping, billing, and accounting for the plant had to continue in his existing system until I could put my own in place. His terms were tough, but he agreed.

On Tuesday, December 21, 2004, I closed on my loan from Chemical Bank, and the KenSa plant officially became the cornerstone of the newly created AG Manufacturing. That afternoon, my accountant and I drove to Harbor Beach, where the icy wind off Lake Huron stung our faces as we approached the hulking, 50,000-square-foot plant. It had once bustled with 120 workers, but by the time I bought it, most of them had been laid off. KenSa had also stripped much of the equipment. When I arrived that afternoon, I owned the building, some equipment, and some old inventory. The nineteen remaining employees were waiting to hear what I had to say. Most expected that the plant would shut down. The former owner had not been very forthcoming with his workforce, but the layoffs and the removal of key equipment spoke for themselves. Many undoubtedly thought that this would be their first and last time meeting the new owner. Not surprisingly, they were not particularly happy to see us.

I stood on the factory floor and silently wished I'd prepared some remarks, but I'd been entirely focused on the closing itself and hadn't yet laid out the details of the case I'd make for these employees.

I said a silent prayer that I would not stutter and said, "Hi, I'm the new owner of the facility. This is my friend and CPA Mike Onianwah. I've never run a manufacturing plant before, but I believe I have a way to turn this place around if you are willing to work with me."

I told them that I believe in opportunity, that I would be fair and honest with them, and that I would be there every day to help get the plant on its feet. I told them there was work out there for the plant and that we just needed to go get it.

When I was finished, the workers looked back at me with open skepticism. I waited for questions, and finally one man asked the one that was on everyone's mind, especially four days before Christmas: "Are you going to make payroll this Friday?"

For just a second, I forgot how nervous I'd felt walking in there and how much I'd personally put on the line to buy the factory. This was a question I could answer.

"You have my word that you'll be paid," I told him, "but it may take an extra day or two to get the funds transferred from Boston to cover payroll." I knew there would be many weeks and months when payroll would come from Boston—from the Asaba Group. Even if everything went perfectly, it would be a long while before the plant would generate any kind of profit.

For years, I had dreamed of finding more excitement and fulfillment in my work. I'd wanted to live and die by my own decisions. Now it was happening, and hardworking people were depending on me. I was determined not to let them down.

I had to ensure there would be no impropriety between the Asaba Group and AG Manufacturing. To that end, Asaba stopped its direct consulting for the auto industry after the Harbor Beach purchase. My friend and trusted colleague Mike Bolger had been working with me at Asaba since not long after we both left the Lucas Group, and he assumed many of the daily operations of the consulting practice so I could focus on the new venture in Michigan.

I was excited and intimidated to roll up my sleeves and put everything I'd learned as an engineer and consultant into practice. It's one thing to be involved in acquisitions on an advisory basis, but it's something else entirely to have your hands on the wheel. This was my first time. I was confident in my track record and strengthened by faith, but I knew there was a tremendous amount of work ahead.

I intended to spend as much time in Harbor Beach as it took to figure out the inner workings of the operation, to find out which products were profitable and which were not, and to streamline the business until every part we produced made money. For the next year and a half, I would spend most of my days in Michigan, and I wondered at the outset whether I'd find myself facing the kind of racism I'd encountered in Huntington here, in this equally homogenous part of the country. Would I have trouble finding a place to stay? Would I be told things were already booked, already sold, or already reserved when people saw me? The sting of finding every apartment I viewed in Indiana suddenly, remarkably rented the moment I arrived still hurt, but it had been years since my experience there.

Things didn't look too promising when, despite the fact that I'm a cautious driver, I got pulled over by the police for the first of many times. I sat with my hands on the steering wheel, my heart pounding, waiting for the officer to take my license. I told him as I handed it over that I was in town for work, that I'd bought the KenSa plant.

For those few minutes I didn't feel like an engineer or a guy with an MBA or the owner of a two-million-dollar factory. I just felt like a very vulnerable black man on the side of a road in a town where I never saw other people who looked like me. I was acutely conscious of my accent, and I spoke slowly and deliberately, breathing evenly to calm my nerves.

After a few minutes, the officer gave me back my paperwork and politely told me to have a good day. It was a scene that would play out time and again. I never actually got a ticket—but then again, I was never doing anything that would warrant one.

Roadside challenges aside, the community welcomed me and chose to put their faith in my vision for the plant. I made a standing reservation at the Franklin Inn in Bad Axe, Michigan, twenty miles from the plant, where the owners gave me an exceptionally low long-term rate and agreed to bill me monthly. On the nights I worked late, they kept the kitchen open so I'd have a hot meal when I got in. When I worked too late for that to be feasible, they'd leave me a covered plate to reheat. I appreciated those plates, with steaks and potatoes and fresh bread when I got back from ten or twelve or more hours at the plant, more than I can express. When I needed high-speed internet to work from my room, the Inn installed a wireless antenna on its roof. I had a matching one installed at the plant. It would be a while before T1 installation was in our budget.

My experience at the Inn was echoed throughout the community. Despite the fact that on most days I would not encounter another person of color anywhere in my travels, I was never treated with any recognizable bias. The community wanted the factory to succeed, and it embraced my efforts to bring it along in every way possible. Before long, people were greeting me by name at local restaurants and shops. Harbor Beach became a second home. This reinforced my confidence, faith, and determination that I was on the right path.

———

The first order of business in turning the plant around was getting a handle on everything it made, what the demand was for those products, and which were profitable or not. It was an enormous task, as the existing infrastructure didn't capture a lot of that information in any useful way. The factory made hundreds of different parts on demand, and there was no effective system in place for tracking the orders and their profitability or for forecasting them for the future. Before we could be successful, we'd need better visibility. We had to create a system that reported based on actual orders. Once I got it working, I could know everything we made during the week by Friday afternoon and have a record of all our receivables by Monday morning. I would start tracking every part to determine which ones were priced to make money. Those that were not would eventually be repriced to be profitable. This was a shift from the way the plant had been run in the past, and I encouraged my team to become more data driven.

In the beginning, I was on-site every day, and I did every job that needed doing—starting with that of sales executive. Every candidate I spoke with about coming on board for sales wanted a retainer, but no built-in contacts or promised business came with those deals, so I started going on sales calls myself. Some days I took on a finance role and dealt with the bank or with the former KenSa owner. Some days I helped address engineering issues, and others I dealt with customer issues and legal concerns. For a time, my permanent address was the address of the plant, and the corporate headquarters of AG Manufacturing was the suitcase full of files I toted everywhere I went. We ran very, very lean at the start.

I'd been working until midnight for years, and I continued to do so. In those first weeks, the plant's employees got used to me being around and seemed to sense that my commitment was genuine. I did my best to be transparent and honest with the information I shared with them. They knew I wasn't drawing a paycheck and that payroll came from Boston every Friday. I had open books. I told all the employees that I intended to run the business based on trust and that we would take care of each other.

In our first full year, 2005, we made $1.2 million in sales, but our costs were $1.7 million. In 2006, we made $2 million and had $1.9 million in costs. The change was slow, but it was happening, and I made sure everyone who was working at the plant knew where we stood and that my determination to turn things around was unwavering.

In turn, they stepped up wherever they could to help implement the improvement plan. It didn't take long to realize that we didn't have all the personnel we needed. For starters, we needed an on-site bookkeeper. One of the plant staffers gave me a phone number for Gail McConnachie, an accountant who had been laid off by KenSa.

I reached Gail in the least likely of places to find a good book-keeper; she was out on a tractor harvesting sugar beets, one of the region's biggest crops. I waited while she shut down the rumbling tractor so we could talk, then asked her if she'd meet me to discuss the possibility of coming back to work. She told me the plant was going to die, but she showed up all the same and agreed to take the job.

Over that first year, I got to know Gail and the other employees: their backgrounds, educations, strengths, and weaknesses. They were going to be integral to my success or failure, and I wanted them to feel as much a part of the turnaround as I did. They showed a tremendous amount of heart and willingness to work with me, but there were some gaps between the skills the group had and what was needed. KenSa had not made training and employee education a priority. I focused on implementing new technologies that would help capture data and automate our processes, and I strove to make training available wherever it was needed.

———————

I learned some hard lessons during my first two years owning the plant. One of those was about just how toxic a negative person's influence can be. KenSa's previous owner proved to be the antithesis of everyone in the community who supported my vision. I don't believe we ever had a conversation where he failed to tell me that my plan to revive the factory would fail. He frequently told me that he was just biding his time until I went bankrupt, at which point he'd take the plant back for pennies on the dollar. He reminded the plant's employees of what he believed was the imminent loss of their jobs, too. They may not have known or trusted me in the beginning, but they all had well-formed opinions of this previous owner, and I think many of them were willing to give me a chance in part because I projected a calm positivity that was unlike what they'd experienced with him.

Another tough lesson came when we got some new business for a school bus company to build wiring harnesses and failed to quote the job properly. We were earning about $500 per harness, but it was costing us about $570 to build each one. We were in the hole on every single bus, but we honored the contract. When the deal expired, I repriced the harnesses to make them profitable for the next cycle. The customer promptly moved its order to Mexico.

Recruiting was also a problem. The town was small, and the community had seen dark days at the plant, so a lot of people were hesitant to come on board with us. It was especially challenging to find a qualified plant manager. I brought in a few people from outside the area to interview, but the typical response after that initial visit was that either the applicant or the spouse wasn't interested in moving to Harbor Beach.

As a minority-owned supplier, we had a competing advantage in bidding some contracts, and I was always acutely aware that I was the only minority player at the plant. When I mentioned to one of my employees that I aspired to hire more minority workers and asked if there were any local candidates, I got a surprising response. Without looking up from her keyboard—in a manner that clearly betrayed no malice—that employee answered, "We don't have many around here, and the ones who come driving around up here from Detroit are just looking for trouble."

I let that sink in for a minute, watching her work at her computer as if she'd simply said, "Good morning," until I asked the obvious question. "Is that what people around here think when they see *me* driving though Harbor Beach?"

"Of course not," she answered, continuing to work. "People around here *know* you."

I didn't know how to begin to respond to that as I stood there thinking of all the times I'd been pulled over while driving in the town and nearby areas.

After more than a year of struggling and capturing data and sending payroll from my consulting firm every week, I was no less determined to make things work, but our situation was grim. The loss on several hundred bus wiring harnesses had been a big blow, and Hal Zaima's constant derision took a toll.

Early in the second year, I realized I would have to either cut staff or trim hours to ensure I could keep us afloat. I called a meeting to tell the plant's employees the bad news. I felt terrible as I gave them my proposal that we would go to a four-day work week until I could make new sales. Having to pay employees for one fewer day each week would make it possible for us to hang in while we generated some receivables. I laid out the numbers—as I'd been doing since the very beginning—so each person would know what we were up against, as well as the vision I still had for turning those numbers around. I told them I would not be able to pay them for Fridays for a few months but that I would still be at the plant working as usual if anyone needed to reach me.

The group took it well. They thanked me for sticking by them and promised to accept the temporary schedule change and the pay cut it would mean.

I had no idea how strongly these employees, whom I'd gotten to know over the year we'd worked side by side, felt about that team until the first Friday rolled around. I went to work as usual—and so did every member of my management team. They all showed up like they had every other Friday and proceeded to put in full a day's work, knowing it would be unpaid.

I couldn't believe it. I had expected to work alone. My faith in the operation had never wavered, but now I knew my faith in my employees had been equally well placed. We were truly a team.

While we were working our way through this difficult time, I got a call from an executive at the Yazaki Group. Yazaki, the world's largest supplier of wiring harnesses, is based in Japan. They'd sent a large shipment of harnesses to the United States by ship, and in the weeks it took for their transport, there'd been an engineering change for the entire order. They wanted to know if we could make the necessary alterations in Harbor Beach.

That influx of new billable work became a turning point. By the end of the second year of my ownership, not only were we back to five-day weeks, but the facility was also supporting its own payroll. We were ready to hire additional employees. A highly qualified local candidate accepted the job of plant manager.

By the end of 2006, the plant was profitable and running solidly in the capable hands of its new manager. I needed him to feel empowered to run the business without me looking over his shoulder, so it was time for me start pulling out of my day-to-day role. I was ready to get back to strategic work. I placed my trust in the plant's team, and they have never let me down.

Before turning my attention to a new venture, I had one last matter to handle. I went back to Doug Herringshaw at Chemical Bank with new records and projections in a new presentation, this one about restructuring my loan. My new objective was a simple one: to pay off the derisive owner of KenSa who had loomed over my first years of plant ownership. With the bank's cooperation, I paid him off two years ahead of schedule. I hoped that cutting ties with the owner, who had disrespected my employees and the company for years as he whittled away its operations and workforce, would be a sign to my team that I had total faith in their long-term success.

Over time, the plant in Harbor Beach became self-sustaining. Today, the facility employs 150 people, and most have good jobs that pay a living wage and provide benefits. After the early, difficult days of getting the company off the ground, I found the emotional income that came from creating jobs and empowering people was just as valuable as the financial income I was finally earning. The fact that the factory was in an often overlooked and underserved area made its profitability even more rewarding. I wasn't just hooked on being an entrepreneur; I was hooked on going to bed at night believing that my work benefited my employees and our community.

LESSON I LEARNED
Trust Is a Necessary Risk

There is an old African proverb that translates to, *If you want to go fast, go alone. If you want to go far, go together.*

Those words were often on my mind as I set about my two-year sojourn in Harbor Beach. I knew from the start that I needed to trust in the existing employees, and even in the larger community, to make it. And I needed them to trust me. Inevitably, that also meant I needed some members of the community to go beyond the prejudices they may have felt when they first saw me and heard me (or first pulled me over in my car).

That was not the first time, nor the last, that I had to take a chance and give my trust. Nine out of ten times, when I sit down for a meeting there's someone who doesn't look like me on the other side of the table. Nothing good comes of me going into any of those meetings assuming there's a bias against me. I offer my trust and respect from the outset of every relationship and hope it will be returned. Most of the time, my honorable intentions are mirrored back to me. When they're not, I accept it as an anomaly and move on.

As an entrepreneur, try to go into each interaction and relationship in a spirit of trust. Trust translates into confidence in your team and partners. Being wise and being willing to take a chance on other people are not mutually exclusive. Together, we go far.

Chapter 10

LOOKING FOR THE WHITE SPACE

Strive not to be a success, but rather to be of value.

—Albert Einstein

As AG Manufacturing in Harbor Beach became profitable, I was able to look back and analyze the steps it had taken to get there. I kept thinking, *This can be replicated.* The business model took time, but it worked. I threw myself into searching for the right opportunity to try again—perhaps expanding beyond the block and tackle work of wire harnesses.

The Harbor Beach facility occupied a competitive white space— an area of unmet need or an industry pain point that lacked an optimal solution. In theory, the parts manufactured at Harbor Beach could be made more economically overseas, but once the time and expense of shipping were factored in, the economic advantage of making them in countries with lower labor costs disappeared when it came to fulfilling immediate demand. The idea of white space investment is that a unique opportunity is there for the taking but somehow hidden in the margins. I was eager to find another one.

I scoured the industry, relying on my consulting background to help me find a good investment prospect. I was good at finding elusive data, and I knew how to apply the numbers I could pull together to find meaning and make worthwhile predictions. On the days I got discouraged, I'd think back to some of the creative and obscure methods I'd used in my time as an analyst to get necessary information. One of the most oddly challenging assignments had been to analyze on-premise beer consumption in a region where there was no sales scan data available. I spent the better part of two weeks going to every beer garden, outdoor club, and popular watering hole, politely requesting that the proprietors save their bottle caps for a month. All of them agreed, and at the end of that time, I hired a small team to gather and count the caps. When we were through, we had all the data we needed to determine which brands were dominating this segment of the market, and my client was able to target it more effectively and grow its share.

I figured that if I could make good use of data from bottle caps, I could surely find an effective investment strategy in the auto industry. The segment was, and is, a massive economic force, with thousands of establishments in forty-some states. There were, beyond doubt, opportunities to be found. I just had to keep looking.

In the end, it may have been my determination to stay local that helped me define an investment niche. I knew that any time I wanted to bid for production work, I'd be going up against far larger companies like Delphi or Continental—places that had a hundred product development engineers to my one or two. Even if I was the lowest-cost guy, I would never win an even race for those contracts. No one ever got fired for giving a contract to a major industry player, but any executive who took a chance on me and my small company would be taking a risk. I needed to be able to compete on some other level.

Harbor Beach gave me the idea of scouring for production lines that were nearing the end of their original equipment manufacturing (OEM) lives and zeroing in on those businesses as they tapered production volumes. It was a unique and potentially profitable segment of the market, because many major industry players are only interested in parts that are in demand at high volumes. When production starts to wind down—for example, when the next generation of a vehicle is coming soon—a lot of big companies start looking for an out. Lower production volumes don't work for the big players, but I thought they could be ideal for me and my smaller operation. I could buy a declining product line, run it profitably to the end of its OEM life, and either continue it in aftermarket for as long as there was demand or replace it with another line. I spent a great deal of time looking for the right opportunity to put my theory in practice.

I found that opportunity in 2006, in Rochelle, Illinois, though it took some imagination to recognize its potential. The factory was also in a rural community, this one about eighty miles from Chicago. It produced actuators and solenoid valves and was profitable, but the product line was scheduled to die out within two years. The corporation that owned it looked at the situation as an exit window. I looked at it as an opportunity with a small window for success. If I could purchase the factory, I'd have two years of built-in profitability until the existing product's end of life—two years to find and bring in a new product to replace it.

I financed through a local bank, finding it easier to get a substantial loan with the Harbor Beach turnaround on my resume. Even before I took possession, I was searching for a way to keep the profits flowing when the two-year grace period the plant came with expired.

The Rochelle plant was a fully equipped, full-scale operation that had a capable staff and good management in place. Many of the employees were mature adults who'd been in their jobs for decades, and they were an efficient team. For the time being, they just had to keep doing what they'd been doing all along for us all to make it. But in the long run, if I wasn't able to bring new work into the plant, they would either lose their jobs or have to relocate. When I went to meet the team, I assured them that my goals were to keep the factory operational for the long term and to keep the work local. I wanted them to know I wasn't looking to double or triple the workforce or to exponentially increase business. I wanted to keep employment steady and turn a profit every year. I wanted stability for all of us. Their response was one of guarded relief and optimism. The group was professional and experienced enough to know that my intentions were just a pipe dream if I couldn't find new work for the plant.

The clock was ticking to find new business for the factory. I had twenty-four months to devise a new way to utilize the equipment, the technology, and the willing and qualified workforce that kept it all running smoothly. After months of researching, putting out feelers, and making sure people in the industry knew I was ready and able to bring a new product line to Rochelle, I heard a rumor that BorgWarner, a major manufacturer, might be looking to divest a throttle body line that was no longer core to its original business. This was a product that could be moved, that the Rochelle facility could capably produce, and that could be expected to be in demand for years to come. Barring any major blows to the auto industry, it would generate enough business to keep the plant profitable.

I negotiated a deal to buy the line, and we were in business for the long haul.

———————

Even as I was buying the throttle body line and getting its production underway in Rochelle, indications of financial strain in the auto industry supply chain were brewing. There were rumors of diminishing profits and impending bankruptcies. With most of my personal wealth and professional energy invested in the auto industry, I was thinking about expanding my business interests into manufacturing in other arenas. I reasoned that because a wiring harness for aviation or other systems is essentially the same as one for a car, I could find a natural area for expansion in manufacturing harnesses for another industry. In addition, with two plants already in the manufacturing heart of America, I was interested in pursuing an investment in the booming South.

I put out the word that I was looking for a small electrical assembly company in a southern state, and one day I got a call from a man named Jim Davis in Wetumpka, Alabama. Jim spoke in a kind, intelligent manner as he told me he'd been asking around about me and that he admired the way I'd turned around the Harbor Beach plant. He also knew I had experience working with the air force through my consulting practice.

Jim owned a company called Quality Networks, and his factory made aircraft wire harnesses and defense component parts on government contract. The business would be secure and profitable for as long as the contract continued to receive its government funding. Jim might have stayed in the business for years to come, but he was sick. After being diagnosed with a serious illness, he wanted to focus on his health and his family. He also wanted to know his company would endure and that his employees would have work security. He said he believed I could sustain his business and asked if I'd be interested in buying him out.

I was honored to be asked and drawn to the idea of taking over a company with a reliable government contract outside the auto industry. After some negotiation, we made a deal. I financed my purchase of the company through a combination of small business loans, loans from a local bank, and personal savings.

Taking over Quality Networks proved to be challenging for many reasons, but the first to come to light was cultural. I had spent very little time in the South and did not give much consideration to how I might be perceived there. On my first trip to the plant, I flew into Birmingham and drove the ninety miles to Wetumpka. Along the way, I passed the Confederate Memorial Park in Marbury. I'd never seen a Confederate museum or Confederate graveyard before. I spent the rest of my drive thinking about the legacy of the Civil War and of how without it, someone like me would never be on his way to take the reins of a sizable local company in Alabama.

I was about to discover that race relations still had a long way to go in some pockets of the South. Just days after my arrival, the plant manager resigned, informing his coworkers that he had no intention of taking orders from a black man. He took a job at a nearby plant—a job with a longer commute that required him to drive past his old office every day. In the week that followed, several other employees followed in his footsteps. At first, I was too stunned at the shortsightedness of individuals who would walk away from good jobs because of the color of my skin to fully process how offensive their reasoning was. It seemed completely illogical.

The previous owner of the company, however, took it personally, calling and apologizing for the behavior of his former employees. Jim said he'd never dreamed anyone who worked for him would react to my takeover with such blatant racism. I was surprised, too, but I felt it was better for anyone who held such a deep bias to clear out than for them to stay and potentially undermine me. I also believed I'd been put on notice that there were those in this southern community who did not want me to get comfortable there.

Starting with a management shortage was an unexpected development, and that meant I needed to spend more time at the facility than I'd planned. I rented an apartment in Montgomery to establish a local presence. I engaged a husband and wife team who worked for me in Harbor Beach to come down and start setting the management tone. Then I met with the remaining management team and with the workers on the floor, outlining my vision for the company with both groups. I made a point to mention there were opportunities for career growth within the company for those who wished to pursue them. It was a small group of women from within the company who answered that call, stepping up and filling the newly available supervisory and management roles with professionalism and enthusiasm. These employees rose to the occasion when I most needed people I could count on and proved themselves to be both capable and trustworthy.

Just as we got the plant functioning under its new management chain, it became apparent that our lucrative government work was going to come to an end sooner rather than later. The parts we were manufacturing supported the war efforts in Afghanistan and Iraq, and those conflicts were winding down. Quality Networks' defense contracts were long-term, but they were funded annually, and as political moves were made to reduce US military involvement in the Middle East, future orders on the company's contracts went to zero. With just the current year's orders to count on, I was about to run out of cash flow to maintain operations. In a matter of months, we were facing no orders, overdue bills, and personnel problems exacerbated by the former plant manager's frequent admonishments to my employees that the plant was doomed and they would all lose their jobs. Sadly, there was a kernel of truth in that warning—it was possible I might soon have no choice but to shut down.

I had known when I bought the factory that the government defense business would not last forever. I wouldn't have wanted it to. But my long-term vision of transitioning the factory to private sector work was suddenly an urgent matter. I needed to find work to sustain the plant, and with the time constraints I was facing, it seemed like my only options were in exactly the sector I'd hoped to keep the Wetumpka investment free of: the auto supply industry. That was the business I knew best and the one in which I was most likely to be able to find salvation for the otherwise doomed plant.

It didn't take long to discover that no major auto company was willing to give an unknown quantity—a defense contractor with no auto experience—a chance. It became clear to me that I'd have to completely break with Quality Networks and its history to have a chance with the auto industry. AG Manufacturing had a growing reputation that I could use to help bring business to Wetumpka. I began to scale down Quality Networks and to ramp up AG Manufacturing in its place. I separated the real estate from the company and transferred employees between the two entities, giving priority to those who demonstrated a willingness and ability to learn a new way of doing business and those who weren't buying into the former plant manager's negativity toward me and my operations. My management team and I did everything possible to ensure continuous employment for those who were committed to sticking with us.

For better or worse, there are vast differences between the way most companies working on government contracts and those working within the private sector operate. With a government contract, the work is guaranteed, and once it is secured neither management nor the workforce needs to feel driven by a sense of competition in the market. In the case of the Wetumpka factory, this truth was magnified. Quality Networks had the benefit of a coveted "sole source" contract, a noncompetitive agreement in which the government reimburses the contractor its costs plus a cost-based fee. Although the intention of these contracts is to provide reliable business to worthy companies, in practice, competitive edge often becomes a nonissue under their terms. If the contractor wishes to make more money, the most efficient and effective way to do so is not by focusing on the finished product but by raising its own costs. In the private sector, this is simply not the case. There, the entire workforce needs to buy in on some level to the idea that operations must be competitive, lean, and poised for growth to survive. I needed to oversee a massive shift in the corporate culture of the Alabama factory if we were going to survive the transition from its dependency on government contracts that were drying up to private sector profitability.

Once again, it was a production recall that got me on the road I wanted to tread. I acquired a contract to do recall work on an airbag wiring harness, which bought me time to find long-term work. Back in my comfort zone in the auto industry, I focused on a familiar angle to give me a competitive edge: shipping costs.

The size of fuel tanks prohibits them being manufactured internationally—paying to ship a tank full of air is simply too costly for most budgets. Every vehicle's fuel tank requires a fuel delivery module, which includes a wiring harness. I focused our efforts on building wiring for these tanks, knowing that if we could combine these two key parts with cost efficiency, we could be profitable. In order to focus potential customers on the benefit of domestic manufacturing, I offered a proposal to a nearby plant that included bringing the harnesses to them, saving the logistics and costs of getting the same parts delivered from Mexico. Not only could I ease the complications of day-to-day operations, but it was also convenient if their engineers and other key personnel needed to visit my facility—no more sending workers to Mexico or Honduras or China to address engineering or production issues.

It took time to make the transition and to get our new business model underway, but in the end the Alabama plant settled into a new normal that worked.

LESSON I LEARNED
Find New Ways to Create Value

There are four key questions to consider before delving into any new business:

1. Can we identify an opportunity or hidden truth that others don't see or believe exists?

2. Is there a specific market segment that we can build without going against entrenched competition?

3. How durable and defensible is our expected market position against competitors?

4. Can we execute on the opportunity and sell others on the concept?

The first three questions deal with identifying competition-neutral zones and defining the white space. Where is the hidden opportunity? Why is a segment of the market overlooked? How can you serve that need? If you can identify an unmet need, an overlooked efficiency, or a better way to get something done, you have the beginnings of successful entrepreneurship. Reduced competition is inherent in the idea of identifying a "hidden" opportunity. Every entrepreneur has to be willing and able to compete, but there's no reason to choose arenas where the competition is fierce if you don't have to. Once you've found your niche, you want to be able to grow and profit within it. If you can't visualize a path to long-term profitability, you're probably better off sitting it out.

The last question goes beyond your ability to see and meet a need and into your skills as a salesperson. One of the reasons many would-be entrepreneurs opt to stay in the corporate world is an aversion to sales. In a corporation, you may be able to achieve impressive levels of success without ever having to make a pitch or ask someone to select you and your product or service over that of the next person. Entrepreneurship rarely works that way. Most of us have to sell to survive. Even after your business makes it big and you hire a sales staff, there will be times when you are called upon to look a customer in the eye and ask him or her to buy in. None of my manufacturing concerns would be worth anything without the customers and contracts that support them, and the only way to acquire those customers and contracts is through sales acumen.

For me, with my accent and stutter and long history of sitting at the back of every classroom, praying I would not be called on, sales ability did not come easily. In order to succeed, I had to take two very important steps. The first was just to accept it. Selling is a reality that is part and parcel with entrepreneurship.

The second, perhaps more important, step I took in becoming a worthy salesperson was completely different—something I recommend to anyone trying to find their way with a new business. I had to believe in the pitch I was making and the benefit I could offer my customer. I am not at all good at deception, and without faith in my own case and proposition, I knew I would fail. I was never going to be the kind of salesman who can close a deal on the strength of smoke and mirrors or bourbon and cigars. Instead, I relied on my biggest strength—analysis—and on listening to potential customers to figure out what their problems were and how I could solve those problems better than anyone else. I had to learn how to clearly articulate my "why buy?" proposition.

Don't waste your time selling something you don't believe in. Figure out how you can genuinely meet a need, and sell that. If you're confident that you are the best possible person to deliver a product or meet a need, potential customers and clients will sense that truth and respond.

Chapter 11

TESTED

It is always darkest before the dawn.

—Proverb

With a growing group of auto supply-chain factories and a path to profitability in each, by 2008, AG Manufacturing was beginning to be a force in the market. But as an entrepreneur, I get regular reminders that there are factors outside of our control, and the biggest one of my career was right around the corner.

There were rumblings of trouble as early as 2006, when Detroit's Big Three automakers began reducing their long-honored commitments to minority-owned suppliers. After more than thirty years of prioritizing those relationships, industry leaders didn't necessarily have a lot of choice. They were increasingly losing US market share to international competitors like Toyota and Honda, and they had to find ways to run leaner. With demand down, some companies started to fall by the wayside. They weren't able to hang on when automakers' orders didn't meet projections. I was aware of the impact industry changes were having and how they were driving the exodus of jobs to Mexico and Honduras, and I was already committed to a lean, carefully designed business model that could succeed. But I could not have been prepared for what happened next.

The global financial crisis kicked off in 2007 by the collapse of the subprime mortgage market was, many economists believe, the most significant financial crisis since the Great Depression. By the time the Lehmann Brothers investment bank failed in the fall of 2008, the financial tidal wave was directly affecting the auto industry, where it would continue to wreak havoc for years. I had defied industry trends by investing in American manufacturing and American labor in the auto industry and had succeeded, but there was only so much pressure and negative impact my businesses could handle. It was not a great time to be committed to revitalizing dying manufacturing businesses—especially businesses that were not yet fully rooted and self-sustaining. My fate was inextricably tied to that of my industry, and before long we were all teetering on the edge of a precipice, peering down at the jagged rocks below.

It started with orders being down—down by percentages higher than any we'd experienced. We worked lean and hoped it would get better. It didn't. People weren't buying new cars. With gas at near-record prices, they weren't even driving the cars they already had very much.

My strong relationship with Chrysler was one of AG Manufacturing's greatest assets. In 2008, Chrysler was responsible for a significant percentage of orders to my companies. But in April of 2009, the unthinkable happened. Chrysler filed for bankruptcy, followed within days by GM. Suddenly my greatest asset was my greatest liability. All of my orders from Chrysler would be halted, and my receivables from them would be held up—and could possibly go unpaid. I had an immediate and dire cash flow problem.

It wasn't just me and my employees. There were close to 750,000 people working in the auto industry's supply chain—nearly three times as many people as worked for the Big Three automakers directly. We were all in financial peril. My own situation was more critical than that of many of my fellow business owners, because I had tied up nearly all of my personal net worth in my manufacturing investments. If my companies failed, then I would fail. Worse, I would lose the small amount of financial security I'd managed to build for my own family.

Whether business was up or down, the banks still held my debt, and most banks are quick to remind business borrowers that they are not our partners. They want their payments every month—no exceptions. There's another aspect of business loans that a lot of people who haven't worked in industry aren't aware of: the fact that a bank can call your business loan due for almost any reason, including an unpredicted economic downturn. You don't have to be in default to have your loan rescinded. Each of my loans contained a clause that stated the bank could recall because of industry conditions.

Both my bank in Rochelle and the one in Alabama chose this path. Fifth Third Bank and Amcore Bank in Rochelle had been heavily invested in the real estate industry and were the first to come for their money. I'd only had the Rochelle plant for about a year when they decided to call my loan. My local Compass Bank in Alabama was not far behind. I didn't have the cash to pay them off, so I had to find a way to repay them without losing the businesses.

My mind raced through options every day, from the time I woke until I went to bed at night. Should I sacrifice one plant? It felt like a betrayal of everything I believed in to dissolve what I'd built and turn my employees away. I thought about filing for bankruptcy. There were times when it seemed that might be the only option I could still exercise.

Instead of giving up, though, I got creative and looked for allies to help reduce my exposure—a plan that relied on two things: the goodwill I had once received with one bank; and a little inspired manipulation of another. First, I went back to Chemical Bank in Michigan, to the team that had given me my first substantial loan. Once again, even in the midst of a global financial crisis, they put their faith in me. Harbor Beach had been enough of a success that they were willing to help refinance my loans in Rochelle. It was enough financial relief to keep that facility going for the near term.

The next piece of the equation was more challenging. I needed to somehow convince my Alabama lenders to work with me. I took the approach that a failure at the AG plant would be their problem as much as mine. I was certain this was the truth. The people who worked in that plant weren't just my employees; they were the bank's neighbors, their customers. The plant was a force for economic good in the community, paying employees who then paid taxes, bought groceries, and frequented local businesses. Whatever short-term good it would do the bank to call my loan would ultimately be mitigated by the fallout—losses on mortgages, car loans, and future businesses—not to mention the eventual payoff of my loan, which wasn't even in default.

At that moment, I was teetering on the edge and needed them to buy in, to work with me. I also needed them to understand that the auto industry moves slowly, but it does move. Every car actively being built already has its suppliers in place. They will not be replaced unless they fail. But every recall, model year change, and program redesign brings new opportunities. My sales efforts were focused on future model years, and I needed everyone involved to recognize that we were looking at profitability not in a matter of weeks or months but in one to two years. I responded to the bank's demand to call the loan by going back to them and insisting that they recognize the realities of the economy and share in the responsibility for this factory in their own community, telling them point-blank, "If you restructure this loan, you'll help save a hundred jobs in this community."

When I recounted my meeting to Mike Bolger, who was still running the day-to-day operations of the Asaba Group on my behalf, he wryly told me I was one of the few people he'd ever met who would always wear down a system before the system wore me down.

Mercifully, in this case, he was right. By putting ownership of the Wetumpka factory back on the lenders, I was eventually able to convince them to refinance my loan with more favorable terms.

––––––––

In each of my factories, we tightened our belts and ran as lean as possible. My plant controller and finance manager shuffled and prioritized bills, juggling to keep us current with lenders and vendors. We continued to build and ship product on time to fulfill our customer orders. Employees and management in each plant pulled together to get through. Privately, I leaned on my faith, praying that I would not have to shutter any of my facilities.

When the dust settled and the auto industry slowly began to recover, many of our competitors had not survived the devastating financial blows. Countless companies in the supply chain went out of business, a fate that many lenders shared responsibility in for having called in their loans. Triana, Plastech, Exemplar, and QC Onics were all manufacturing businesses like mine that didn't survive.

In time, the industry began to revive and raise production levels. Those of us who were still in business were able to take on more work and breathe more easily. We had successfully weathered the storm.

LESSON I LEARNED
Don't Let a Crisis Go to Waste

I don't know anyone who has been successful in a straight line. Even if you're on an upward journey, there will always be valleys along your way. Part of being a successful entrepreneur is accepting the fact that business is risky. You can't control all the variables. There's no magic trick to lift you up and over hard times. You just have to trust there is a way and get to work finding a solution.

As an entrepreneur, you will inevitably experience failure and unfairness. When something goes wrong, don't wallow. Don't let your pride or hurt feelings get in the way of your recovery. Learn your lesson so you never fail at the same thing twice.

If you've never been an entrepreneur or are just starting out, when something goes wrong, you may be inclined to go into mourning. Don't waste your time. Failure is not the opposite of success. It is an integral part of the process of achievement. There's always an important lesson to take away. Be crafty, and figure it out. Learn it well so your crisis doesn't go to waste. One of the best pieces of advice

I ever received was simply this: If there's no way around a crisis, fail fast. Find your feet. Then move on.

Chapter 12

INTEGRITY

*To be yourself in a world that is constantly trying to make
you something else is the greatest accomplishment.*

—Arianna Huffington

n manufacturing, no matter how good or how prepared you are,
you're always at the mercy of break-even volume. There are many
substantial fixed costs—things like property and machinery—
that must be covered regardless of production levels. For example, a
facility capable of producing 10,000 widgets in a week might have
to sell the first 4,000 to cover fixed costs. If your customers decide
they're only going to take 3,000, you're in trouble. There's no way
around the demands of break-even production.

Because of this fiscal reality and the troubled state of the auto industry, I was thinking a lot about investing in another industry with an entirely different business model. Branching out from your core business can make or break an entrepreneur, as some choose to invest in areas where they are not knowledgeable or nimble enough to be competitive, while others find security in holding diverse assets. One of the things that had long interested me was the prospect of doing business not just in the United States but also internationally. And the idea of investing in a consumer branded products business was hugely appealing, because anything in that realm would have remarkably low fixed costs compared to the three facilities under the AG Manufacturing umbrella.

A few other auto industry entrepreneurs were thinking along the same lines, and a peer of mine who had a condo in the same Detroit building I lived in had invested in the startup of an up-and-coming beverage brand called Cintron. Wes Wyatt and I met to talk about possible collaboration and made a deal. I would own the rights to take the product into Africa and hold the Cintron trademark there. I could utilize my business contacts in Nigeria and South Africa to get things started. I felt the deal represented minimal risk for me, that the most I could lose was product. I was also eager to help create a unique image for the brand and forge an innovative marketing and distribution plan. I had a lot of ideas about launching the product as a high-end label and tying its publicity in with my charitable interests. It seemed like an ideal opportunity to explore a new industry and to focus on finding a way to make the customer want to spend more rather than ceaselessly chasing costs.

I started building the brand in Africa almost immediately, establishing distribution channels, making plans to introduce Cintron at events, and signing Grammy-nominated artist and producer Akon as a brand ambassador. As the business began to take off, one of my employees went to a law firm in South Africa to get paperwork pertaining to the trademark, only to be told by the attorney's office that they had just spoken with my office in Philadelphia about finalizing trademark ownership.

I didn't have an office in Philadelphia. But my partner in the venture did.

Afraid I was being double-crossed, I flew to Detroit for a face-to-face meeting. Wyatt denied filing for the South African trademark. I wanted to believe that was true, but further investigation proved his agents had filed not only in South Africa but also in Nigeria. My easy, low-risk business collaboration was about to turn into a legal and professional nightmare.

I owned the brand in Africa and had invested substantially in its success, but now I was going to have to fight for it. As Wyatt and I ramped up a battle over the brand, I felt I had no choice but to stop buying product through him and so found myself, despite my best intentions to steer clear of it, setting up my own manufacturing arrangements.

What followed was a years-long battle that showed me a side of business interaction I'd been fortunate enough to avoid until then: using character assassination to gain a competitive edge. My disagreement with Wyatt and his company, Cintron Beverage Group (CBG), was a professional one, but they were quick to devolve into personal attacks. Their tactics included always referring to me as "this Nigerian man" or to my "Nigerian associates" in legal documents and letters in an attempt to focus attention on my race and heritage—despite the fact that we were two American businessmen who had made a deal in Detroit. The CBG team insinuated that I had stolen their trademark. They used deliberately intimidating language with obviously threatening undercurrents. They even sent a process server to my house to bang on the door when they knew my family would be at home and I would be working in Michigan.

In business, you must choose your battles, and I have never been above losing a skirmish or ceding some ground to win a war or reach a greater goal. But in my dealings with this company, my character and integrity were repeatedly impugned, I had been threatened, and the sanctity of my family home had been violated. It felt as if everything I had done from the day I arrived in New York until this moment was being called into question. Was I the straightforward, hardworking American veteran and businessman I believed myself to be? Or was I the dishonest, manipulative outsider they were depicting? I believed the outcome of the litigation would either clear or permanently stain my reputation. And based on that belief, I was unwilling to cede any ground.

Even as the turmoil around my Cintron beverage business unfolded, my other interests—Asaba Group and AG Manufacturing's plants—still needed my attention. My ability to put on my game face and get on with the business of being a leader and a decision-maker for my companies was tested.

My faith was tested, too. There were times when I had to just stop what I was doing and pray for patience or strength or guidance and wisdom, but I always continued to believe that this matter, which had become much more than a business problem, would be resolved and that I would be vindicated.

At one point, I felt so threatened that my lawyer was compelled to document the threats to my person as a record in case any harm came to me. But giving in was never an option. I was prepared to fight as long as necessary.

After two years of litigation, stress, and working against an enemy I had never dreamed I would have to face, the end came at the hands of a federal judge in Philadelphia. Judge Sanchez flatly dismissed all of the claims against me. The ruling was made "with prejudice," meaning the false accusations and incriminations I'd faced could never be resurrected in the courts. I walked out of the courtroom feeling a great weight had left me, that I could reclaim my life, my business interest, and my focus as I put the adversity of the experience behind me. My office issued a press release announcing that we had won and that I was willing to vigorously defend against anyone who attacked my character.

In the months that followed, I bought Wyatt and CBG out of their remaining dealings with Cintron and acquired the global trademark. Wes and I made peace. My foray into a simple distribution investment had been a long, complicated and unpleasant journey, but now I was free to build the brand as I imagined it and to take it worldwide.

LESSON I LEARNED
Personal Integrity Matters

Without personal integrity and the kind of social capital that can only be earned by delivering on commitments, my path to entrepreneurship would have ended before it had truly begun. I would never have been able to found a successful consultancy, never earned the opportunity to write the industry papers that set my team and I apart, never been able to land big government or private sector contracts, and never been able to secure the financing to buy my first factory.

Building a reputation for being reliable and trustworthy is lifelong work, and it is critical to entrepreneurial success. For better or worse, people—prospective investors, lenders, partners, employees, customers, and suppliers—will judge you on the basis of your character, your history, and your word.

In business, things often move so fast that your associates may only be privy to an initial narrative against you. If that happens, you have no choice but to go to war to regain control of your story and your reputation. You can defend your integrity through direct rebuttal and also by leveraging press releases and other communications to ensure that your customers, stakeholders, and business partners hear your truth.

I am not inclined to engage in frivolous fights or to waste time or energy waging war with adversaries, and I don't recommend that for any aspiring entrepreneur. In a perfect business world, each of us could focus on innovation and strategy, delivery of our objectives, and building relationships. But we don't live in a perfect world, and there are times when even the most goal-oriented and focused among us will be shaken by underhanded moves, dirty business maneuvers, and personal attacks. Someone will eventually try to knock you down. What you do next is up to you.

One of the most impactful speeches I've ever heard was Denzel Washington's 2017 NAACP Image Awards acceptance speech. In it, he stressed the importance of hard work and consistency. "Keep working. Keep striving. Never give up," he said, then continued, "Fall down seven times. Get up eight."

Get up eight. I'd been knocked down before my battle over the Cintron trademark, but I had never been hit quite so hard or so unexpectedly as during that conflict. That made it all the more important for me to not just get up but to fight.

Chapter 13

INNOVATION

It is better to risk boldness than triviality.

—Peter Thiel

With the auto industry meltdown in the rearview mirror, I was determined to finally follow through on my aspiration to take a controlling interest in Sid Taylor's SET Enterprises. I had served on the board since 2004, when he and I first discussed the prospect of me playing a role in the company's legacy plan. But I had not been in a position to amass the resources to buy 50 percent of SET and gain board control. In fact, I'd taken on a great deal of debt investing in an industry that had come close to flatlining.

By 2012, however, AG Manufacturing was stable and profitable. We were paying down our debt, and we were growing. Despite the hardships of the previous years—and contrary to the advice of some of my trusted colleagues—I believed it was the right time to double down on the auto industry. The reasons were threefold. First, SET would change the scale of my portfolio and operations. With operations in four states and annual revenue approaching $350 million, it would more than quadruple the holdings under my direction. This was not organic growth like everything I'd done before. It was a big move, and I believed its time had come.

Second, SET had an extensive, established network in the industry. I would have a new level of access to relationships with both customers and suppliers—relationships that Sid Taylor had cultivated over decades. If I could ensure that SET continued to deliver as it always had, I could potentially leverage those connections throughout my organization. In some ways, I would be buying a seat at the table in the industry.

Third, and perhaps most important, I believed that SET was ripe for innovation. Its steel processing business was highly competitive, undifferentiated, and with declining margins. The business model was running out of steam. After spending more than a decade as a consultant and an investor, always looking for opportunities in the white space, I'd started to dwell on the idea of moving beyond just identifying what was underserved. I was inspired by the kind of innovation that led to the founding of Southwest and Amazon and Uber, companies whose leaders found a way not just to modify but to actually create new business models and reinvent industries. I believed there was potential at SET to fundamentally change the existing business model to create a more sustainable company and assure its long-term growth and become a value stakeholder it the communities we it had facilities.

The primary business activity of SET was steel processing. The essence of the work involves using massive presses to form, cut, and stamp flat-rolled steel into shapes used for doors, pillars, floor panels, and other outer panels of vehicles. This simple, mechanical process has remained unchanged for decades. Every time I discussed the process with friends and colleagues, I came back to the same question: Why are we still tied to this process? Taking the helm of SET would allow me the opportunity to explore other ways—and perhaps to find something that would be more cost-effective, more open to customization, more agile, and more efficient.

In August of 2012, I acquired controlling interest in SET and began my new role as its president and CEO. I was about to start answering my nagging questions about its operations, to see if it was possible to evolve our mission from press-cutting steel—which had been done the same way for decades—to the utilization of advanced technologies and the incorporation of lighter metals. To make it happen, I'd need to have buy-in at all levels of the company, from union shops to factory floors to executive offices. I traveled to each facility, meeting workers and managers. At each, I explained my vision and enthusiasm for introducing new processes and innovations to established ones. I discussed with employees and the management team about how automakers would increasingly be looking for lighter materials and about how SET needed to be ready for them. Moreover, I shared my belief that rapidly evolving technologies like 3-D printing, robotic lasers, and machine learning could and should have a direct impact on the way we planned to do business.

Eventually, our mission gelled into the intention to utilize three different emerging technologies that would help move the process beyond the antiquated mechanical systems of the past. We were prepared to be early adopters of state-of-the-art programs that were just starting to emerge and to be innovators in our own right. Rather than continuing to compete only on a level field with all the other companies who were doing the same kind of work as SET, we were going to offer something completely different. In an industry niche that has literally been defined by immutable dies and presses for decades, we were going to offer agility and flexibility. When discussing this sea change with my team, I frequently used the age-old comparison that the maker of the first light bulb wasn't focused on making a better candle. The innovation was only possible when the focus was on the greater need: illumination.

I also reminded my teams that the best way to ensure sustainable jobs is always sustainable profitability. We weren't looking to grind out just a miniscule edge against our competition, constantly existing in a "fourth down and inches" mentality. We were looking to offer something no one else had—to make ourselves indispensable to our customers.

While many of our competitors continued to operate the same decades-old presses and processes, SET began moving forward with investments in new technologies. Today we are encouraging our customers to design parts on their computers, send them to us in real time, and have them made exactly to their specifications without costly and time-consuming die creation. Utilizing lasers, robotic arms, proprietary software, and a host of other innovations, we are becoming capable of producing superior-quality products at higher production rates than were believed possible even a decade ago.

Importantly, these new systems work equally well with all grades of engineered materials, so as the auto industry looks to make cars lighter, our technology is just as applicable to aluminum alloys, magnesium alloys, and various other high-strength alloys as it is to steel. Automakers have taken notice, and while we've maintained our established relationships in the industry, we have also forged new ones with companies like Schuler, Arconic, ArcelorMittal, and Novelis.

For me, these early years with SET have been a reawakening. After a long time hunkering down, focused on riding out the recession and fighting my legal battle, turning my attention to SET's complex combination of analysis, management, and leadership needs has created a new professional energy. Some of it is fueled by the opportunity to get back to my engineering roots. Some is the chance to be on the cutting edge of new industry developments. Some is facing the challenges of running an increasingly large and diverse organization. And as ever, some of my enthusiasm comes simply in knowing that each of my companies is creating and sustaining jobs— that I am fulfilling my greatest responsibility as an entrepreneur.

LESSON I LEARNED
Question Mental Models

We are living in an age of innovation, a time when technological changes are making things possible—in design, production, communication, and nearly every other area of business—that have the potential to change our lives and our industries. Twenty years ago, markets were much more static; an industry was a chess board, with clearly defined hierarchies, boundaries, and rules of engagement. A diligent and creative entrepreneur could study the board and identify a neglected niche—a white space—and stake a claim there. But today, in our digital age, competition and market boundaries become more fluid every day. Rather than simply confining our attention to white spaces or to the potential opportunities in their margins, disruptive entrepreneurs are identifying opportunities above, below, and off the grid in all directions. This may be the most opportune time in history to question existing mental models—an age when almost anything is possible.

The auto manufacturing industry represents a perfect microcosm of the impact of these developments, as time-tested processes are augmented and sometimes challenged by original, even disruptive inventions and ideas. In my industry, we see vast changes every day in things like increased production and efficiency and new career paths, often juxtaposed with companies and careers that fail to keep up and become obsolete.

Sometimes an entrepreneur's best path is a traditional one, following in the footsteps of those who have been successful before him or her. But equally often, opportunity is found in innovation and technology, in new ideas, in doing something in a new or better way than anyone before you. The essence of technology is to enable us to do more with less. Emerson wrote, "If a man ... can make better chairs or knives, crucibles or church organs, than anybody else, you will find a broad hard-beaten road to his house, though it be in the woods."

Much of my professional success is directly attributable to analyzing all the factors in existing businesses in search of improvements and to reimagining business models in ways that might work better. Analysis can get you a long way, but remember that if you actually do build a more innovative crucible or church organ or mousetrap, investors, partners, and customers will indeed beat a path to your door.

Chapter 14

RAISING ALL BOATS

Real wealth is not defined by if you can pay
for it but if you can pay it forward.

—Sekou Andrews

n 2012, I traveled to Nigeria to attend a Cintron-sponsored event and visit my father and extended family for a few days. At the end of my trip, I arrived at the Abuja airport with my documents in hand, ready to travel on a Dana Air flight to Lagos, where I'd connect to a Delta flight bound for Atlanta and then Boston. At the check-in counter, I stood behind two men who were given their boarding passes and sent on their way. When it was my turn, the agent informed me I was too late to make the flight. I was sure there was still time and refused to be turned away, telling him, "I *have to* be on that plane."

The agent held his ground as I protested, finally saying, sternly, "Sir, you are not listening to me. The flight is *closed*. It is too late."

An hour later, I was sitting in the airport, still working on my alternate arrangements, when a group of people watching a television nearby started shouting and crying. The flight on which I was refused boarding had crashed into a building in Lagos on its approach. Before long, there was footage of the crash scene on every TV—a horrific, flaming tangle of airplane and brick and mortar, with chaos all around it as locals crowded the site, trying to make sense of the wreckage and help if they could.

Tragically, there was no one to help. All 153 passengers and crew on my flight died in the crash; ten more people were killed on the ground. It was the second-worst air tragedy in Nigeria's history, and I had been turned away at the gate.

I have always been mindful of God's blessings in my life: a loving family, a quick mind, a healthy body, and so many opportunities. Many times, when it seemed I had reached a point where there was no way to go ahead, a door opened for me: my tuition paid, a loan approved, a crisis survived. That day, a door was closed. I was denied, and as a result my life was spared.

I spent a lot of time in the days after the tragedy thinking about mortality. My brother and I sat down and talked about it, about people we knew who'd been weighed down with regret and fear at the end of their lives. I have never been shortsighted about legacy, but the events of that day still made me want to reassess, to make certain that when my time does come, I'm not caught wishing I'd lived my life differently. I want to live a life of significance, and when the time comes, I can say I live the life I intended.

The question I kept coming back to when it came to my role in the business world was this: *How do I fundamentally ensure that my daily interactions are meaningful?* I wanted to recognize my opportunities to change other people's trajectories for the better—for a day or for a lifetime. I believed, then and now, that my legacy as an entrepreneur would not be measured in how many companies I led or how much money they made. It would and should be assessed on the basis of whether I helped the people I could help and whether I contributed to some greater good than personal gain.

———

So, how do you change another person's trajectory? In my experience as an entrepreneur, it's often done by offering an opportunity: a chance at an education, a job, a valuable connection in an industry. These are the avenues of professional success, and an entrepreneur can offer access to them.

I try to always give unique consideration to those who, like me, might not immediately project the assuredness or pedigree of a shining star prospect. He might have an accent, or she might have gone to a less-regarded school than other applicants. They may have qualities that make it easy to identify them as outsiders. Often, these are talented people who simply need someone to give them a chance.

One of these was Isabelle, a young woman who applied for a professional job at the Asaba Group during its early years. Despite her extensive education, when I met her she was working a minimum-wage retail job in a mall. Isabelle had an accent and a degree from a foreign university, and so she'd been overlooked for job after job because of her nontraditional background. When we spoke, I was impressed with her analysis ability—enough to offer her her first professional-level position. Isabelle took that job and ran with it.

She excelled at every task she attempted. In a few short years, she'd outgrown the position and the company, eventually landing a VP position at a major Boston investment management firm. She was a stellar prospect from the start. All she needed was for someone to open one door.

Sometimes bending someone's arc comes in the form of standing by an employee. Over the years, I've had many employees put their faith in me during difficult times, and I strive to return their confidence and kindness. When a young employee who'd worked for me since high school was in a terrible accident, we kept her on regular salary throughout her recovery. When executives who had sacrificed compensation and vacation stayed with me in the early days at Harbor Beach, I made sure to show my gratitude when the company stabilized by breaking out my personal checkbook. When employees—young and not-so-young—have expressed an interest in higher education, I've supported and sponsored their studies. As the scope and scale of my business has grown, I've taken steps to institutionalize these gestures into corporate policies wherever possible, in the hopes that they'll still be available even when I, personally, am not.

At times, the most impactful positive influence comes in the form of mentorship, and at others, it comes as an investment. Occasionally it's both, as was the case with a young entrepreneur I met while attending a Cintron-sponsored charity event in Johannesburg. Steven was a smart, charismatic guy creating an up-and-coming lifestyle brand. We got talking and hit it off, and soon he was peppering me with questions about entrepreneurial ideas and directions—a favorite topic of mine. We stayed in touch, and one day he reached out, looking for advice on a business crisis. An investor who'd committed to supporting his company wanted out—immediately—and like most entrepreneurs, Steven had those funds tied up in the enterprise. Refunding the money would put him out of business. He was vulnerable and struggling to find a solution.

I had a lot of faith in Steven's promise as an entrepreneur. He was intelligent and driven, and he'd shown heart and integrity in our interactions. So I asked him what he needed, and I wired him the funds. Because we hadn't talked terms, he believed I was taking a controlling interest in his company—something he was willing to abide to save it. But going down that path would have taken away his professional autonomy, and I felt there was a better way to structure our relationship. Instead of an ownership bid, I suggested a long-term sponsorship. Steven would plan and execute events for my company in the years to come, and the funds that bought his emancipation from his investors would be a down payment on that work. I didn't want to be an investor in his business; I wanted to be an investor in his success.

Steven never let me down, but of course when any of us takes chances on human nature, occasionally we lose. I've done my best to provide needed funds in the form of assured continued business to a number of aspiring entrepreneurs, and most of those arrangements have benefited both their businesses and mine in the long term. When the rare disappointment takes my money or fails to follow through, however, I accept that as a part of the risk of doing business.

One of the things I deeply believe and try to impart to up-and-coming entrepreneurs is that each of us who makes good must remember the opportunities we were given and the people who took a chance on us. We have a moral obligation to extend a helping hand to the next generation of men and women willing to work hard and take chances to follow the American dream of business ownership.

I believe that I cannot afford to make money that doesn't make change, and in addition to my personal commitments, each of my companies follows through on that promise, engaging in charitable pursuits that range from supporting organizations that empower underprivileged children in Detroit to hosting international events to raise awareness of human trafficking or raising funds to promote awareness of testing and early detection of breast cancer in communities of color.

In recent years, as Steven and other entrepreneurs I mentor come back to me with increasingly optimistic and enthusiastic updates about their companies' prospects, I'm mindful of the day Father Borgognoni comforted me in the chapel at Syracuse, the day I found out my tuition would be covered for another semester, the day Courtland Cox gave me the chance to distinguish myself with an industry paper, the day Doug Herringshaw closed his office door and told me I'd get my loan—all moments that changed my trajectory. Herringshaw's words will always stay with me. "Look son," he said. "I believe in you, and I believe in what you're trying to do."

I have come full circle from those days. Now it's my turn to show a little faith.

LESSON I LEARNED
Play the Long Game

Over the years, I've been asked how I put myself through school, or weathered the recession, or came out ahead in my battle for the Cintron trademark. The crux of the answer is simple: I played the long game. I was going to sweat it out, no matter what. It didn't matter if it was harder, if it took longer, if I had to grit my teeth in anger or bow my head in prayer. I was determined enough to look past the near term—a hard day or trying weekend or even a challenging year. I would wash cars or hold doors or take a lesser-paying job or tighten my belt and ask my employees to do the same. When things got difficult or even ugly in the moment, I centered myself and looked further ahead to my objectives: a life-changing education, factories employing hundreds of workers with their doors still open, a hard-earned professional reputation. They were all worth fighting and striving for.

Playing the long game is equally important in relationships—with customers, suppliers, employees, colleagues, and even friends—as it is with goals. So often, I meet people who are determined to get the most out of a single transaction, even at the expense of the relationship. That's naïve. None of us can afford to be shortsighted and alienate allies. In business, your relationships should not be measured in transactions, but rather in years and even decades. Over the years, my associates who were self-centered and rushed in their dealings have nearly all flamed out. But those who stayed steadfast, who built and strove, who prioritized goals and relationships over immediate gratification—they're still here. That kind of commitment has a way of compounding itself over time. When the going gets rough and you've survived a few storms, you know what to do. You know how to get through. You have the resources and the allies and the trust equity necessary to overcome almost any hardship.

Becoming an entrepreneur—the kind who betters his or her community and raises all boats—means building something solid and sustainable. As you build a business and foster relationships, always remember to play the long game.

EPILOGUE

O n June 21, 2017, I traveled to Washington, D.C., as part of a delegation of African American CEOs and business leaders. There, we met with members of Congress and representatives from the White House. Among the dignitaries who joined our group were Department of Commerce secretary Wilbur Ross and Minority Business Development Agency director Chris Garcia. Garcia holds the same post today that Courtland Cox held in 2000, when he gave me my first small but important government contract. I was terrified the day I met Director Cox, but he saw past my nerves and awkwardness and gave me an opportunity. This year, I met the MBDA director as the head of a holding company that has 800 employees and revenues approaching $500 million a year. In the seventeen years between those two meetings, I have truly lived the American dream.

Over the years, it's become evident to me that my best investments—those most in line with that American dream—are those that serve a purpose above and beyond personal and corporate wealth creation. America has been good to me, and my life here inspires my ever-deepening patriotism. The spirit of citizenship is something very dear to me, and I consider the livelihood of my fellow citizens and our collective communities to be a shared responsibility. Today, I own eight plants around the country, all of them in underserved neighborhoods, most of them once at risk for closure and the elimination of living-wage jobs in places that sorely need them. In each case, I looked at the investment in terms of how to bring business back, save jobs, and how to get revenue flowing again.

In a world where corporate responsibility is becoming a priority among a growing segment of executives and business owners, I often meet other business leaders who share my beliefs. Among these are decision-makers who recognize the way I'm trying to do business and want to participate, invest, or do business with my companies. We fundamentally agree that true entrepreneurial success is measured by far more complex metrics than how many dollars you can earn in a day, a year, or a lifetime. Entrepreneurs have a responsibility to create jobs. Employers have moral obligations to their employees and communities.

At times, my journey of American entrepreneurship has been difficult. At times it has been lonely. At times, it has been so dark only my faith gave me light. But I've kept that faith—in God, in the essential goodness of people, and in the core American values of hard work, persistence, and ingenuity. It is a combination of all these things that makes entrepreneurship an opportunity to lift up not just one person who takes a risk to create or save a business, but everyone who is touched by that enterprise. We are all metaphorically at sea together, we must all stay afloat together, and be equally committed to raising all boats!

ACKNOWLEDGMENTS

Delving into my life story for this book was a powerful reminder of how many people I have to thank for my success.

Those who gave me a shot: Jay Lucas, Courtland Cox, Jethro Joseph, Doug Herringshaw, Burt Jordan, Keith Cooper, and Sid Taylor.

Those who worked with me: Michael Bolger, Jeff Symon, Chelsea Brehm, Shamsudeen Bello, Gail McConnachie, Betty Thrash, Kevin Schwanz, Rick Campbell, Chris Ubosi, and Anand Moodliar

Those who stood by me: Katrice Edozien, Michael Onianwah, Gil Edozien, Renee Wesley-Case, and Richard Kruger.

Those that prayed with and for me: Mom, Annette Edozien, and Chelsea Brehm.

Those who helped me achieve my goal of publishing the story of my American journey: Jana Murphy, Frankie Edozien, and Antoinette Turner.

ABOUT THE AUTHOR

VICTOR EDOZIEN is the chairman and CEO of both SET Enterprises and AG Manufacturing and the managing partner of Asaba Group Holdings, his private equity holding company. He is an expert in growth strategies and corporate turnarounds. Victor fundamentally believes in the free-market economy and entrepreneurship as vehicles for creating jobs that uplift communities. Victor is a veteran of the US Army and a Wharton Fellow at the Wharton School. He holds a BS in electrical engineering, a BA in geology with mathematics, an MS in engineering, and an MBA in finance and operations management. He is a member of Young Presidents' Organization, the Entrepreneurs' Organization, and CEO Connection.